CW00858747

First Printing, 2017

ISBN 9781520289625

Book one in the Rockingwood Stables series

For my wonderful friend Sammi

Long may your adventures continue

1981-2010

Chapter One

Sophie

"Hey! Horse face!"

Sophie Scott froze in her tracks at the familiar, harsh voice that called out from behind her. Her hands started to shake and her breath quickened. She knew if Carly Johnson and her gang noticed her panic, it would make her even more of a target. She shoved her hands deep into the pockets of her dark green jacket and tried to take deep breaths. Pretending she hadn't heard, she braced herself, but carried on walking toward the school gates, praying the girls would lose interest.

Then it happened. The same thing that always happened. One of Carly's gang, a tall plump girl named Katie, barrelled into her from behind. She stumbled and fell to the ground. As she fell, she dropped her bag and the history exercise book that Sophie had carefully decorated with horse stickers fell out. Hoping they wouldn't notice the stickers, Sophie shot her hand forward to grab it. Before she could, a glittery black shoe suddenly came down upon her hand. Sophie gasped. Her hand was stuck. She looked up and saw that the shoe belonged to Carly. Who else would have such a glittery shoe? Even at the end of the day, Carly's uniform was pristine. The jewelled clips in her long, golden hair shone like her shoes. She looked the complete opposite from Sophie, who was so plain looking, with her own long brown hair tied up in a pony tail and the same plain black shoes she had worn to primary school last year. Sophie's hand was throbbing, but she refused to give the gang the satisfaction of seeing her yelp. Carly's blue eyes were staring right at her. Sophie looked down nervously.

Why did they have to pick on her just because she loved horses? Carly yanked her history book out from under her hand, causing Sophie to bite her lip in pain.

"How sad is this book?" Carly quipped to the other girls. They laughed. It was an intimidating sound. "Plain, boring, stupid horses. Just like you." Carly went on, throwing the book to the ground. Before Sophie could grab it, Katie, the plump girl reached down and hauled Sophie painfully to her feet. "Eww don't touch her Katie," another of the gang cried, "she even stinks like a stupid horse."

Menacingly, the gang laughed and Katie shoved Sophie away from her, holding her nose with one hand as she did so. Before the girls could do any more, a teacher came into view. With one last threatening glance over their shoulders, the girls marched away, giggling as they went.

With shaking hands, Sophie pushed her now muddied history book back into her bag and climbed unsteadily to her feet. "Are you OK Sophie?" boomed one of the teachers from behind her. Sophie's heart sank.

Now all eyes in the playground turned to her, drawing attention to her predicament. Sophie knew she would never admit to what was happening to her. She would be even more humiliated if her parents or friends were to find out.

"I just tripped. I'm fine." Sophie lied before heading once more out of school. As she neared the school gate, she looked around cautiously in case Carly and her gang were waiting for her. She couldn't see them, so she made a final sprint toward safety on her school bus.

Once on the bus, Sophie drew a tissue out of her bag and began madly rubbing away at the muddy patches on her knees. She had to get rid of them before she got home. The last thing she wanted was for her mother to notice and start asking awkward questions. As the bus set off, Sophie lost herself deep in thought. All year at school, Carly's gang had teased her constantly. They'd labelled her love for horses as being weird. They'd told her she was a loser for playing with horses when they were doing *'proper'* sports like hockey and net ball. Carly Johnson had been the most awful. Sophie wished she didn't exist.

Carly had been the worst part of Sophie's life ever since she'd started in year seven. To get to know each other, the children had been asked to bring in

items that were special to them. One of Sophie's items

was a picture of her sat on top of a chestnut pony whilst

on holiday with her family in Wales. Carly Johnson had

snatched the picture from her hand and scoffed at it.

Laughing, Carly had told her that she wouldn't be seen

dead in a pair of navy blue jodhpurs and had loudly told

the class that she stunk of horses. Sophie had always

been shy and nervous, so this really hadn't helped her to

make many new friends in her new secondary school.

The other girls had seemed drawn to Carly and her loud

attitude. Sophie wasn't drawn to her at all though. In

fact she tried to avoid her. Sophie hated the way Carly

and the others made her feel scared and made her face

flush a hot, embarrassed red.

On Carly's say so, the other girls excluded Sophie

from groups on the play ground and left without a partner in lessons. In a way, she sort of knew they were better than her.

Carly was the star player of the school netball team. It was expected that she was going to be the team captain in year eight. She was so stylish too and always turned up to school looking glamorous. There was no wonder that all of the other girls wanted to be her best friend. Sophie had some friends of course, but she didn't dare admit to them how the gang made her feel. She was sure that they wouldn't understand the way that she felt lonely and constantly embarrassed that she was never good enough for anyone else. How could they? Sophie was the only one amongst her group of friends who had always gone horse riding and so she was the only one who had been the victim of the horse taunts at school. Her other friends were a bit more normal and so were able to get along much more easily in school. Charlotte was her only friend who could understand Sophie's passion for horses. Sophie sighed. If only Charlotte had been there to walk with her after school, Carly's gang would have left her alone. Only Charlotte, being her usual impulsive self, had been asked to stay behind to talk to the teacher after class after being caught pulling a silly prank on one of the boys in class.

As the bus made its way toward her home village of Branton, Sophie sighed. Horses were the one thing that Sophie was really good at. Horses would certainly never make her feel bad or lonely. They were such kind creatures. She had started having lessons at the age of five and had spent only a few months needing to be on the lead rein. When she was on a horse, she felt free, like she could do anything. Deep down she knew she wasn't the bravest of riders, but lots of people had told her she was a natural. It was the only thing that ever boosted her confidence.

As soon as Sophie jumped off of the school bus, she dashed straight home. Calling out a quick hello, she ran straight upstairs to change out of her muddy trousers and hide her muddied history book. Once her bedroom door was closed behind her, she breathed a sigh of relief. At least tomorrow was Saturday. She smiled at the thought of attending her weekly riding lesson at Rockingwood stables. Like many pony mad children, she longed for the week to be over to spend one wonderful hour with the beloved horses and ponies there. Saturday wasn't only fantastic because Sophie could spend time with her beloved ponies; it was also the day of the week where she could forget about all of the unpleasantness from school. It wasn't like she tried to put school behind her when she was around horses. It was more like school seemed like a different life. She still felt anxious that she wasn't good enough and she certainly didn't dare ask the owners of the stables if she could spend some extra time with the ponies. But she felt free when she was around the horses. They were so gentle and kind toward her. She could truly be herself, relax and feel happy. In a way, she knew she was lucky to be able to live this entirely separate and happy life. She was well aware that not all children had such an easy time of it getting away from the school bullies.

Sophie settled down in her bedroom. She had indulged her love and brought some peace to her life by surrounding herself with all things horsey. Posters of all types of breeds of horses and ponies and of famous riders covered the walls of her bedroom and her wardrobe doors. She admired the posters of the famous show jumpers the most. She could just imagine the thrill of popping over the incredibly high fences and cantering off with a red rosette and huge, glittering trophy.

Sophie had a rosette of her own, a large blue and white one that she had won in a knowledge type quiz in one of her many pony magazines. She smiled fondly, remembering the surprise when the large envelope had arrived with the rosette and a letter congratulating her on winning second place. Even now, she couldn't believe she had beaten all of the other children to win a prize! It wasn't quite the same as having won a rosette with a trusted equine companion, but she had still felt the thrill of finally having won a rosette and proudly displayed it in her bedroom. One day she would be the one cantering around with a rosette proudly pinned to her pony's bridle, even if it was only in her dreams.

The next morning was much brighter than the day before. Just like Sophie's mood. She leapt out of bed and began to pull on her worn, navy jodhpurs and bright blue top, which her mother had relegated from 'best top' to 'riding top' only. Even though it was faded, Sophie had insisted on continuing to wear it, as the black horse's head on the front reminded her of her favourite pony at the stables, Sammi.

Sammi was a mischievous jet black pony, with a white star on his forehead and two small, white socks on his hind legs. A real dream pony. Pulling her brush roughly through her long, brown hair, Sophie quickly scraped it into a ponytail, it wasn't perfectly styled like the girls at school, but she didn't care. Dashing down the stairs, she just hoped that she would be allowed to ride Sammi this morning.

The family's kitchen was a large space, with a breakfast bar to one side. Sophie thoughtfully laid out bowls for everyone, even
 her older brother James. He too thought she was stupid for loving horses, which really didn't do anything to help her confidence, but then he knew nothing of the way the others at school treated her.

Making a mug of tea, Sophie settled herself on a stool with her favourite chocolate cereal and a pony magazine. It wasn't long before she heard her mother come down and poke her head around the door.

"Having breakfast?" she asked with a smile.

"Err, yeah. We need to be at the stables extra early this morning," Sophie replied impatiently.

She hoped her mother hadn't forgotten what an important day it was and quickly breathed a sigh of relief when she saw that she was already dressed. For the first time ever, her best friend Charlotte was coming with her to the stables. Even though Charlotte was popular with many children at school, she was a real friend to Sophie. Charlotte was certainly the only friend who understood and shared her love for horses.

Together they would sit in Sophie's bedroom for hours, flicking through the pages of glossy horse magazines and learning everything they could from a mountain of horse books they had collected. Charlotte though had never been allowed to learn to rider herself. She'd never even really been around ponies. Sophie couldn't wait to share her favourite ponies with her friend. She hoped the stables would be quiet if they arrived early enough, so that she could take Charlotte around and introduce her to all of the horses and ponies, especially Sammi. She smiled to herself as she imagined Charlotte agreeing with just how beautiful the pony is. It also wasn't the only treat in store for Charlotte today, Sophie and her mum were planning to give Charlotte her birthday present a few days early.

As Sophie waited by the car with her riding hat in her hand, she sent a quick text to let Charlotte know they were on their way. Finally they were driving down the twisting country lanes towards Rockingwood. They would pick Charlotte up on the way. She lived in a cottage just two minutes down the road from the stables.

Sophie couldn't imagine how anyone could have lived so close to so many ponies for so long and not have visited them. Staring out of the window, Sophie watched the horses in the fields they passed as they left their village of Branton and started heading towards Rockingwood. She sighed, wondering what lucky girls must own them. Glimpsing a small palomino and a larger skewbald, she imagined stroking her hand over their soft muzzles, hopping up onto their bare backs and galloping freely across the paddock. She would hold on tight to their flowing manes, knowing no-one was around to tell her otherwise, she would pop over the fallen branch at

the far end of the paddock and whoop with exhilaration.

"Sophie...Sophie! Stop daydreaming."

"Huh?" Sophie replied. She shrugged off her fantasy ride

and realised the car was slowing down.

"We're here," her mum told her as they pulled into

Charlotte's driveway.

Sophie leapt from the car and swiftly crunched across

the gravel, eager to collect Charlotte as quickly as

possible.

Chapter Two

Charlotte

Sleepily, Charlotte Barker rubbed her eyes and sat up in bed. She had tossed and turned for most of the night and not dropped off to sleep until the early hours. She wasn't sure whether it was the excitement of finally being allowed to accompany her best friend Sophie to the stables, or the anxious knot that had formed in her stomach about doing just that, that had kept her awake all night.

Charlotte wasn't used to feeling anxious about anything. She was usually so confident and sure of herself. Her mother had often marvelled at just how much energy and enthusiasm Charlotte had for everything in life. Stifling a yawn, Charlotte decided that the only thing for her to do now was to get up and get ready to see what the morning had in store for her. She wasn't going to hide away underneath her duvet. Really, she ought to get a move on. Sophie and her mum would be here to collect her in half an hour.

Rummaging through her wardrobe, Charlotte decided on a pair of black leggings, an old, faded t-shirt and a dark green hoody.

She didn't have a glamorous pair of jodhpurs like the other girls would have and hoped no-one would make fun of her. She'd seen the way some of the girls at school made fun of others for not having the things they had. She knew how unkind Carly Johnson was to Sophie and although Sophie would never admit it, Charlotte secretly looked out for her friend where she could.

She reasoned with herself that the people at the stables were probably going to be really friendly. After all, these were the most suitable clothes she had.

She sighed as she fastened her long blonde hair into a tidy ponytail, wishing the anxious feeling would go. Today should have been the most exciting day of her life. Charlotte had longed for so many years to be close enough to a pony to stroke it and let it nuzzle her hand. She had always imagined that their muzzles would feel soft and smooth, after all they didn't seem to have much fur here.

Until she had been two years old, Charlottes mum had had a horse of her own. Although Charlotte couldn't remember him, she had seen pictures in an old photo album that her mum kept underneath the coffee table as a keepsake.

The horse had been a handsome dark bay welsh cob gelding of about 15 hands, named Ted. When she was younger, her mum had told her how Ted had proudly carried the tiny Charlotte on his back and safely walked around the paddock of their old house with his precious load on board. Her mum had just three photographs of Charlotte riding on Ted. Charlotte had spent many hours over the years pouring over the photographs and could see from the pictures how happy she had been to be on the horse's back.

As she had gotten older, Charlotte had tried not to look at the photographs too often. Even though she loved to see them, they reminded her of the fact that she wouldn't be able to enjoy riding a horse ever again.

She had always had a burning desire to be

around horses and to learn to ride, she supposed these pictures and her mother's stories had been inspiring her from a young age. But it just wasn't possible. Not long after the happy photographs had been taken, Charlotte's father had been killed in a tragic accident. Her mother had been devastated and to make it worse, she had had no option but to sell her beloved Ted to make ends meet. The family had been forced to move from their house with a paddock, to the small cottage they lived in now. Her mother had taken a job as a taxi driver so that the family were able to get by. Charlotte did what she could to help her mum when she wasn't at school, however she could tell that her mother was almost permanently exhausted from all the hours she did at work, whilst still looking after everyone.

Charlotte and her two brothers were happy

though. Her mother, knowing how much Charlotte had loved horses,

had often taken her for walks where they could see the horses over the fence of some nearby paddocks. She had even suggested that Charlotte ask if any of the owners would like some help to look after them. Knowing that her mum would never be able to stretch to paying for lessons, Charlotte had always said no. She couldn't bear the thought of being around horses and never being able to ride. Or to fall in love with a pony only for its owner to no longer need her help and then she would lose the pony, just as her mum had lost Ted. Instead she had thrown herself into playing for the school netball team and looking after the family's three pet rabbits, Ginger, Buttons and Fluffy. Recently, she had bought a rabbit harness with her pocket money and had been teaching the rabbits to jump around a course of fences made from garden cane. She knew she was kidding herself when she had insisted to Sophie this was nothing to do with the show jumping pictures the girls had obsessed over. She knew Sophie probably didn't believe her protests, but she was still a bit too embarrassed to admit the truth.

Creeping down the stairs, Charlotte was careful to avoid the creaky floor boards so as not to wake her mum. She didn't want her to get up and make a fuss. She would feel more anxious if her mother started fussing and she didn't want to feel any worse than she already did. Charlotte decided that she needed to pull herself together. Today would be fine, she was sure. The visit to the stables would probably be great. It didn't really matter that she would never ride. In a way, she knew that this thought was both childish and selfish, but she just couldn't help feeling that way. Charlotte knew that she needed to enjoy every second she had at the stables. It might be her only chance. Not to mention that Sophie was going to be thrilled to introduce her to her favourite pony, Sammi, and she was certainly curious to meet this dreamy sounding pony. Charlotte was sure this was the same pony that Sophie had complained was so naughty throughout the last two years in their old primary school. Now though, Sammi was all that Sophie had talked about for months! Yes she smiled to herself as she heard Sophie's mother's car pull up outside, today is going to be great!

Chapter Three

Rockingwood

Jumping out of the car, Sophie quickly directed Charlotte towards the stable yard. The girls crunched across the gravel car park, making their way through a covered barn, where hay was neatly stacked and into the old, stone stable yard. Charlotte stopped to take in the scene. There were around 20 stone stables, forming a 'U' shape around a cobbled stable yard.

Each stable door was painted a deep burgundy, although many of the doors looked worn, where bits of paint had flaked away. She hadn't expected the yard to look so old fashioned and quaint. Most of the stables she remembered from the pony magazines that she had eagerly thumbed through at Sophie's house had been wooden. This was like something out of a story book.

Some of the doors had heads of all sizes and colours poking over them. She recognised the colours from the pony magazines too.

There was a chunky piebald face looking out from the furthest stable and a sleeker dun nearby. In one corner of the yard was a tack
 room, the door was hooked back and Charlotte could just catch a glimpse of the shiny black saddles inside. She wondered to herself how many people would be lucky enough to ride in one of them today. She couldn't remember herself what it had felt like to be seated in one. All of a sudden, she was aware of a well dressed, middle aged woman striding towards them. She wore and immaculate pair of burgundy jodhpurs that

matched her thick, plaited burgundy hair. It was a warm day and she wore just a polo shirt that was tucked neatly in, with the words 'Rockingwood Riding Stables' picked out in gold and smartly circling a horse's head.

"Good morning," the woman greeted them cheerfully.

"Hi," Sophie replied and Charlotte noticed a familiar shyness creep into her friends voice. "Umm this is my friend I told you about, Charlotte. She's come to watch my lesson."

"Nice to meet you Charlotte, I'm Helen, the owner of Rockingwood Stables. I'll be teaching your lessons today. Why don't you girls go and say hello to the ponies, it's another twenty minutes to your lesson Sophie."

Charlotte wondered to herself what Helen had meant by 'lessons' but this thought was cut short by her friends reply.

"Thanks Helen, we'd love to. Won't Jane mind us looking around?"

"Of course not. Just don't get in her way. She's busy getting the ponies ready and some of the helpers haven't arrived yet." Helen told them as she strode busily away towards the tack room.

"Why would anyone mind us being here?" Charlotte asked cautiously.

"Jane's the head groom, she knows everything about horses and is the best rider," Sophie explained, "She's just better than everyone."

Charlotte just shrugged, she wasn't really interested in some know-it-all. In fact, she wished Sophie wasn't so bothered about what other people thought. She didn't mention anything though. Now she was here, she couldn't wait to meet the horses. The anxious knot in her stomach had turned into excited butterflies.

Walking up to the first stable door, Sophie tentatively held out her hand to a sleek looking dun of about 14.2hh.

"This is Rosie." She told Charlotte. "I've had a couple of lessons on her."

Charlotte stretched out her hand and let the pony sniff her curiously. It seemed like the natural thing to do when Charlotte began to whisper to the pony and rub her neck fondly. Sophie wondered how Charlotte always seemed so confident and at ease with the things she did.

She'd not been around horses since she was a toddler and yet she already looked like she spent every day with them. Moving along the row of stables, Sophie introduced

Charlotte to a larger, smart looking chestnut called Penny.

"Is she a thoroughbred?" Charlotte asked her.

"Erm I think so, how do you know?"

Charlotte grinned, "I read every page of your pony books."

Sophie laughed, "Well be careful, she's really grumpy. Only the most experienced riders are allowed on her and she can bite!"

Charlotte looked at the fine horse and noted how her eyes seemed to be flecked with white and her ears, although not pinned back, were

hardly in what she thought of as a friendly position. Suddenly, she was less keen to stretch out her hand and stroke the horse.

"Maybe you can show me Sammi now," she said, trying to sound eager and hoping her friend wouldn't notice her nervousness.

Luckily, Sophie was too excited about showing off Sammi to notice how Charlotte was feeling. She didn't need asking twice and dashed down to the bottom of the yard and into a little alcove that housed three stables. Once their eyes adjusted to the dim light, the girls could
 make out three ponies in the small stable block. Sure enough, in the first stable was a shining black pony of about 13 hands. His delicate black ears pricked at the sight of them. Unlike Penny, his face seemed to smile a friendly welcome at his visitors.

"Charlotte, meet Sammi!" Sophie exclaimed.

"Wow," Charlotte breathed at the sight of the beautiful gelding and soon started to giggle as he madly began to lick her hand.

She noticed how the marking on his forehead formed a perfect star shape between his eyes and the corners of his lips seemed to have a speckled pattern.

The pony was straining over the stable door to reach the two girls. It seemed a little high for him, though Charlotte supposed this was due to his small size.

"Shall we go inside and play with him?" she asked of her friend.

"Lesson riders aren't normally allowed in the stables," Sophie explained, once again seeming nervous.

"Helen did say you could show me around. Don't be so worried about that know-it-all Jane," Charlotte replied, trying to sound confident.

"OK, I guess you're right, it can't hurt going inside," Sophie decided as she slid back the bolt and knocked the kick bolt open with her foot.

Once in the stable, Sophie made absolutely sure the door was shut behind them. The last thing she wanted was to be in trouble for Sammi escaping. She had heard the girls who helped out say he was naughty for running out of his stable at every opportunity.

Knowing he wouldn't be running free, she turned excitedly to her friend. She could see that Charlotte had instantly taken a liking to the pony. She quickly showed her Sammi's favourite place for a scratch, right by his withers. The pony repaid their kind attention by madly flapping his lips against Charlotte's arm.

"Hey!" she giggled, "That tickles."

"He's grooming you, I think he likes you!" Sophie told her, feeling a pang of jealousy. Sammi had never groomed her like that.

"Do you get to groom the ponies properly?" Charlotte asked her, oblivious to her friend's sudden discomfort.

"No, only Jane and the weekend helpers groom the ponies for the lessons. I'd love to, his coat is so glossy and smooth. If the ponies aren't used for the next lesson, we do get to lead them back to their stables. That's how I found the spot he likes scratching," Sophie replied, the few stolen moments she shared with the pony each week were heaven. Just him and her making friends, it was perfect. "I can show you how to pick his feet up if you like though?"

"Go on then."

Sophie bent down, running her hand from the top of Sammi's silky, black leg. Nothing happened. She'd heard from the helpers that he could be stubborn, but had never really had the chance to pick his feet up herself before. She gave a little tug at the short feather at the bottom of his leg and sure enough he lifted his leg for her. In a flash, the pang of jealousy she'd felt a moment before left her. This was awesome, spending these extra few precious minutes of quality time with the best pony ever. Gently, she placed his foot down in the thick straw bed.

"He's such a good boy, I can see why you like him so much!" beamed Charlotte. She fished around in her pocket and pulled out a polo. Sammi neighed gently and took the treat as quickly as he could, leaving a wet patch of dribble on Charlotte's hand. Both girls looked at each other and giggled.

"Ouch!" Charlotte yelped all of a sudden, "He bit me!"

Before Sophie got the chance to reply, Jane rounded the corner and dumped a saddle on Sammi's door.

"Have you kids been giving him treats?" she asked sounding annoyed.

"Umm well..." Sophie didn't really know what to say, she knew they were in trouble now.

"You shouldn't even be in there. It's not safe when you clearly don't know what you're doing. Anything could happen," Jane scalded them as she brushed her short, icy blonde hair out of her face, "lesson riders should wait by the school for safety."

Sophie could feel her cheeks burning and she looked down at the floor. They'd blown their chance now to spend some time with the ponies. It had started off so well too. Even Sammi had jumped and flashed his ears back at Jane's harsh tone.

Sophie nervously began to trace a circle on the floor with the toe of her jodhpur boot. She hated messing up and getting into trouble. She didn't know what to do now that Jane was so mad about Charlotte getting hurt.

"Come on, let's go." Charlotte said kindly, turning to take her friend by her arm.

Charlotte quickly steered her back out of the small stable block. As she turned to look back at Jane, she realised the pony in the next stable had come to the door to look at the commotion. In clear view, she noticed the pony was a strawberry roan.

She'd seen one just like it in Sophie's magazine and had quickly decided this was the most breath taking colour she had seen. She walked with Sophie back across the cobbled yard, only half paying attention to her friend as her mind stayed with the fascinating roan pony. Charlotte knew that her friend would be feeling worried by the confrontation they had just had with Jane. However, she didn't share Sophie's nervous nature. She knew that no matter what this bossy Jane said, she would have to find a way to sneak back to the stable before they left. She just had to find out what it was like to run her hand over the speckled, almost pink coat of that pony.

Chapter Four

The Lesson

Picking their way back across the car park, the girls met Sophie's mum by the outdoor arena. She smiled as they approached and Sophie could see that she patiently held her riding hat in her hand. Sophie could barely look at her mum as she worried about what had just happened.

"Did you enjoy fussing the horses?" Mrs Scott enquired brightly.

"It was ok." Sophie shrugged, managing a half-hearted smile.

"Sophie...I thought you were so excited?" Her mum sounded worried now.

"Sammi bit my finger and then this Jane came and said we weren't allowed in the stables." Charlotte babbled honestly, before Sophie could protest.

Sophie groaned inwardly, she knew her mum thought horses were dangerous, the last thing she needed was anything that might put her off letting her daughter have lessons. She was relieved when her mum chuckled as Charlotte wiggled her finger about in front of her.

Before her mum could probe for any more details, Helen ambled into the school leading Sammi. She was quickly followed by Jane who led Rosie and two older children who Sophie knew to be weekend helpers; Leanne who led a small 11.2hh chestnut gelding named Casper and Jake who led a 13.1.hh coloured gelding called Eddie. Sophie's heart sank as she saw Eddie. He was a sweet pony but had a reputation for being a bit of a plod. The last time she had ridden him, it had taken all of her effort to kick the pony on into trot. She really didn't want to show herself up like that today, not in front of Charlotte.

The riders booked in for the 9 o'clock lesson all started to shuffle forwards. As well as Gabby and Joe who normally rode in her lesson, there was a younger girl who Sophie didn't recognise who called forward first to ride the smallest of the mounts, Casper. Helen called for Gabby, who was the tallest, to go over and mount Rosie. That left Sammi and Eddie. Sophie held her breath, praying that the next hour would be spent with her favourite pony. Joy swam through her as her silent prayer was answered and Helen announced that she would be riding Sammi.

Walking quickly but quietly across to him, Sophie gave him a gentle pat on the shoulder and hoped he had forgotten the unpleasantness of before. He stood quietly with his ears pricked and alert as she put her foot up into his stirrup. She had only recently learnt to mount from the ground and was grateful to have Helen holding on to the opposite stirrup to balance the saddle for her. She was careful to point her toe backwards to avoid giving him a dig in the side. One, two, three she counted in her head and sprang up into the saddle. He was only 13 hands but she felt like she had just mounted something the size of an elephant. Perhaps mounting was something she would improve at with practise she told herself.

After Helen had helped her to adjust her stirrups, she gently kicked the pony on into a walk around the outside track of the school. She was relieved to see that Jane was busily leaving the school and wasn't moving to watch from the viewing space, especially seen as that was where her mum and Charlotte were now watching her from. Sammi settled into an easy stride behind Gabby on Rosie.

She tried to guide him into the corners of the school but the cheeky pony promptly ignored her and continued to walk in the faint track that was worn around the outside track of the school. Sophie smiled. This is what she loved about the pony. His stubborn determination to do as he pleased, whilst being full of energy and eager to work.

Sophie heard Helen call for the ride to move forward to a trot. With one little kick, the gusty pony sprang forward into a trot. Although his pace was much choppier than that of some of the more elegant horses, he went forwards willingly. As the riders made their way through a figure of eight and a three loop serpentine, Sophie caught glimpses of poor Joe having to work really hard to keep Eddie trotting. Despite Joe constantly kicking his legs, the little coloured pony kept grinding to a halt or casually plodding along at a walk. Sophie heard Helen shout to Joe to give Eddie a little tap with his whip rather than to keep kicking his legs. She felt a little sorry for Joe, she knew that was easier said than done. Eddie really worked his rider hard whilst not giving a willing ride in return.

One by one the riders were told to move their

ponies into a canter until they came

around to the back of the ride. Sophie was now third in

the line, behind both Gabby and Joe. Gabby made

cantering the majestic dun pony look effortless and

slipped back into an easy trot before she met the back of

the ride. Again poor Joe struggled to move Eddie

forwards into canter. For Sammi who was behind them,

this seemed to only agitate him. The more Eddie was

reluctant, the more Sammi pulled at the bit and tried to

stream forwards.

Trying not to panic, Sophie sat up straight and

held on to the reins. Sophie could see that Helen was

focused on encouraging Joe with the stubborn pony and

wasn't really sure of what to do with Sammi. She pushed

her heels down deep into her

stirrups, trying to balance herself. Unfortunately, this seemed to have the opposite effect and sent the pony hurtling forwards. He surged forward, practically at a gallop as he whooshed past Eddie and bolted around the outside of the arena.

Tugging as hard as she could on the reins, Sophie gasped as she tried to slow the runaway pony down. It was no good, he was just far too strong for her. As they hurtled down the long side of the arena, Sophie realised she was going to bounce right off the side if she didn't do something soon. Imagining how she had seen event riders stood up in their stirrups as they galloped around the cross country course, she decided to gingerly lean forwards in her own stirrups. Immediately she stopped bouncing. But now they were rounding the corner,

Sammi's hooves thudding at a tremendous rate as they approached the back of Casper.

Sophie continued to tug on the reins with all her might, but it was no good, any second now, they would surely plough into the back of the tiny chestnut pony. Suddenly, out of nowhere, Sammi screeched to a halt, swerving at the last second to avoid a collision, his back legs seeming to momentarily slide underneath him on the sand. Sophie, who had still been crouched forward in her stirrups, was thrown unceremoniously against Sammi's neck. In a moment of horror, she thought she might tumble right over his shoulder and madly grasped her arms around his neck. Once they both seemed to be still, she tentatively righted herself in the saddle and looked sheepishly around. Joe was lolloping along in a steady canter on Eddie. Everyone else was staring at her. She felt her face, which had been a panicked white only seconds ago, begin to burn a bright red.

"Sophie, are you ok?" Helen called as she dashed towards where Sammi was now stood.

"I think so," she replied sheepishly, "Sorry."

"Now now, don't worry. It's not the first time he's done that and it won't be the last. He can be a real naughty pony when he wants to be. You did well to stay on him." Helen told her kindly.

Sophie didn't feel like she had done well. She felt embarrassed to have lost control in front of everyone and although she would never admit it, she had felt scared. Her heart was still hammering inside her chest. Sammi had never frightened her like that before. Relief flooded through her when Helen called the ride to a walk and they spent the next five minutes working

individually at a trot through some school movement.

Sammi seemed to settle back down now, although his

black coat still glistened with sweat from his adventure.

Sophie was so engrossed in keeping the pony steady, she

never noticed Helen putting up a small cross pole.

"Come around everyone." Helen called as all the riders

made their way to form a line near the middle of the

school. "We're going to take it nice and steady, one at a

time over the cross pole. I'll be standing with you Sophie

to make sure Sammi doesn't get over excited again

whilst he's waiting for his turn.

Gulping, Sophie managed a smile in Helen's

direction. If Sammi had played up about cantering, what

would he be like jumping? Sophie had only started

learning to jump a few months ago and had only been

allowed to jump on some of the quieter ponies. Despite the fact that she idolised the famous show jumpers in her posters, the thought of jumping in real life made her feel nervous. She couldn't say anything. People would think she was a wimp. Especially Charlotte, she wasn't scared of anything. She cast a glance in the direction of the viewing gallery and saw Charlotte watching with fascination as Joe was preparing to jump first. As she saw her friend looking over, Charlotte threw her a grin and a wave. Sophie couldn't let her down now. She had to jump.

One by one, the other riders popped over the cross pole. Gabby cantered Rosie forwards and sprang neatly over the fence. The proud dun pony swished her tail in delight. The young girl on Casper went next and steadily eased over the jump. By the time Joe took his turn, Sammi was beginning to paw the ground impatiently and Helen held on to the side of his bridle, reminding the pony he

had to stand and wait. Joe seemed to go in slow motion as Eddie moved reluctantly forward into a trot. He seemed to almost grind to a halt before lazily stepping over the poles.

Now it was her turn. In a way, Sophie would rather have gone first to get the jump over with. She tried not to let her hands shake as she turned the pony away from the group of riders in the middle. Breathing deeply, she knew if Sammi sensed how nervous she was, he would play up even more. Squeezing her legs carefully, she urged the pony into a trot, although he soon stepped automatically into a canter. Sophie began to relax as the pony went forward calmly and at a much steadier pace this time.

Rounding the corner at the top end of the arena, Sophie turned to face the jump. Sammi pricked his ears and snorted in delight. Before she knew it, he was racing ahead toward the fence, picking up speed as he went. Sophie's heart sank. Once again she realised she was quickly losing control as the panic

rose inside her. Don't be stupid she told herself. Just stay with him. One, two three she counted in her head. Jump! Although, she

wasn't quite quick enough and didn't quite keep up with the pony's bold jump. A sudden thrill shot through her as she realised how gutsy the pony was. He cleared the jump by miles. He must have looked magnificent!

Before she knew it, he had dropped automatically back to a walk and they were heading back to the group of riders in the centre. With a renewed confidence, Sophie was delighted with the remaining ten minutes, where each of the riders were able to have another two, wonderful attempts at the fence.

As she dismounted and ran her stirrups up, Sophie felt relieved with herself for not having submitted to her fear after the nightmare gallop. She even felt a little pleased with herself: Helen had said she had done well. Whilst she found praise difficult to take, she knew she had done well. Other riders might have fallen off and yet she hadn't, she had even gone on to jump! Turning to face the handsome black pony, she gently kissed him on his soft muzzle.

"Thank you" She breathed softly under her breath. For weeks she had dreamed of sailing over a fence on Sammi. She had heard that he was one of the best jumpers at the stables and had thought it would be months

before she would be good enough to jump him. He really had been a dream, soaring over the fences with much more enthusiasm than any of the steadier ponies she had jumped. Grinning, she turned to look at her mum and Charlotte.

"Wow, you looked amazing, I got some brilliant photos on my phone!" Charlotte called, returning her grin, "You must be the best rider here!"

At this last part, Sophie felt her face turn red, she hoped no-one else had heard. It simply wasn't true and so she offered an awkward smile in return.

"You can put Sammi in his stable if you want, we don't need him in the school again until this evening." Helen called.

Dashing over to her side, Charlotte seemed enthralled by what she had just seen. Sophie had almost forgotten the surprise, which was just minutes away, as Charlotte peppered her with questions about the mad gallop and the jump. She was still in a dream about it herself. Seeing that a group of ponies were about to be lead through the covered barn, Sophie directed Sammi the long way back to his stable.

Once inside, she was quick to unfasten the pony's girth and gently slide his saddle off. She knew to hang his saddle on the rack outside of his stable. The mischievous pony had a reputation for chewing on it otherwise. Only as she turned to slip back inside to remove the bridle did she realise that Charlotte was in actual fact looking over the next stable door.

"Where's this pony gone?" Charlotte enquired, seeming almost despondent .

"Maybe someone is riding her in the next lesson?" Sophie replied. She didn't have time to ask why Charlotte wanted to know. It suddenly hit her. The next lesson! Charlotte! She hurriedly gave Sammi one last hug and kiss before turning to dash out of the barn.

"Quick!" she cried, "We have to get back to the school!"

Sophie didn't stop in her speedy exit from the yard and back toward the school. Not even as she felt

Charlotte's eyes boring into her as if to say 'we can't

leave the ponies yet!

Chapter Five

The Surprise!

Charlotte couldn't believe that her friend was hurrying her away from the stables like this. She thought she'd come to meet the ponies. There had barely been any time for that, even though she had patiently watched Sophie's lesson. Now she was rushing her to leave! Maybe she shouldn't have agreed to come after all. Hurrying to keep up with Sophie, she could see she was heading back across to the outdoor arena to her mum. Perhaps they still had to pay or book another lesson, she thought to herself. Charlotte frowned as she drew to a halt beside her friend, not feeling good natured enough to say anything. It was Sophie who turned to her first. She seemed oblivious to Charlotte's annoyance and was in actual fact beaming.

"We have a surprise for you!" Sophie squealed with excitement.

"A surprise...?" Charlotte tailed off, wondering whatever she could mean. She looked to Mrs Scott whose face betrayed nothing of what this could be. Even as Helen approached them and told Charlotte to try on a black velvet riding

hat, she wondered what could be happening. Why did she need to try on a hat for size? Surely she didn't need a hat to stroke some ponies in the yard?

"Happy early birthday!" Sophie announced, grinning madly. "You're having a riding lesson!" her friend explained, looking like she was going to burst with excitement.

"What?" Charlotte stammered, suddenly feeling overwhelmed. Surely this couldn't be happening to her.

"You'll be riding Bonnie today." Helen told her, gesturing towards the magical strawberry roan pony she had seen in the stable.

"The strawberry roan?" Charlotte asked tentatively. Surely this was too good to be true!

"Yes. I see you've done your research." Helen said laughing as she wondered towards the pony.

"Oh wow!" Charlotte exclaimed, grabbing hold of Sophie in an unrestrained hug. She suddenly felt very guilty for the bad thoughts she had harboured towards her, only moments ago. "Thank you, I can't believe you've done this for me!" she gasped.

"Go" Sophie instructed her, "Before you miss your chance." They turned to see Helen was waiting by Bonnie, beckoning Charlotte over to her. She didn't need telling twice!

Fastening the hat on her head, Charlotte strode towards the waiting pony.

"Bonnie." She breathed. She felt shivers run down her spine as she ran her hand down the pony's soft, speckled neck. Bonnie turned her head towards her and nuzzled her hand with a gentleness that Charlotte hadn't felt from the other ponies. "How did you know she's my favourite?" she asked, turning towards Helen.

"Favourite?" Helen said quizzically. "Hundreds of people have started out learning to ride on Bonnie." Helen explained, "She'll look after you."

"Oh." Charlotte responded, feeling a little sheepish. Of course they'd put her on a safe mount rather than just letting her ride the most beautiful pony.

Her stomach churned with excitement as one of the helpers, Leanne, showed her where to put her hands as she talked her through the leg up she gave her. Sitting quietly in the saddle, Charlotte concentrated on carefully gathering up the reins as Helen and Leanne adjusted her stirrups.

"Have you ridden before Charlotte?" Helen questioned as she noted how Charlotte had correctly picked up the pony's reins.

"No, but umm I read a lot of books and watch videos." Charlotte told her as she recalled how she had sneakily watched a video that demonstrated how to hold the reins when riding a horse, when she had been in Mr White's computer class at school.

Helen kindly explained how Leanne would be leading her to help her control the pony whilst she was learning. Looking around, Charlotte noticed how the other four riders in the arena were also being lead. Her heart sank slightly as the realisation struck. She wouldn't be galloping freely around or springing over jumps as Sophie had. Riding was something people had to work hard at to learn over time. Time she did not have. She would just have to work ten times harder than anyone else to make the most out of this hour of paradise, she told herself determinedly.

It felt natural to settle into the pony's long stride as Leanne coaxed Bonnie forwards around the school. Once everyone was walking in line, Helen instructed them to walk through a figure of eight. Although she had heard this in Sophie's lesson, Charlotte was not sure of what this meant and looked quizzically down at Leanne.

"We get the ponies to change rein twice, by riding two twenty metre circles and changing direction over the centre line." Leanne explained.

Charlotte gulped. She was sure she had read about these things in her pony books but it all seemed so much more confusing in real life. Her face betrayed her confusion to Leanne.

"Don't worry, we start with beginners by just changing the rein from B to E twice." she went on.

Looking around, Charlotte found the letter 'B' half way down the long side of the arena. Taking a deep breath, she prepared herself to pull hard on Bonnie's left rein to make sure she didn't need any help in turning the pony. Bonnie swung hard to the left as she

turned to walk towards the 'E' marker. Charlotte gasped as she was momentarily left behind the pony's movement. She hoped no-one had noticed but she wasn't so lucky. Helen asked the riders to halt while she patiently explained to Charlotte how to use her reins and legs more subtly to turn the pony. Charlotte blushed with embarrassment but said nothing, she was still determined to work extra hard to improve. Sure enough, ten minutes later after the riders had worked through a series of figures of eights and serpentines, Charlotte felt much more confident at turning the pony. Leanne was beaming up at her, seemingly pleased with how well she was riding. Charlotte eased her hand off the rein to rub Bonnie's soft neck.

"Well done girl." She whispered and smiled with delight as her delicate ears flicked towards the sound of Charlotte's voice.

Charlotte was so blissfully happy, she hadn't realised that the ride had only been walking so far. She looked over at Helen in surprise at her next instruction. "Now then everyone, we're going to trot one at a time to the back of the ride. Remember to put your inside hand on the saddle to steady yourself and try to keep your legs still."

Charlotte watched with eagle eyes as the other riders kicked their ponies into trot and listened carefully as Leanne explained that she should rise 'up, down, up, down'. When it was her turn, she gave Bonnie a determined kick and was surprised at how the little roan pony jumped into a trot much more easily than the other ponies. It was much bouncier than it looked.

Charlotte found that her legs seemed to swing back and

forth underneath her and Helen called out for her to

hold on to the front of the saddle with both hands to

stop her outside hand moving up and down with her as

she rose. This seemed to help her to keep her legs stiller

and she soon settled into Bonnie's stride. By the time

they approached the back of the ride, Charlotte was

rising to the trot much more easily. Although, she was

relieved when Leanne took control in easing the pony

back to a walk.

"Wow!" she grinned, "This is better than it looks!"

After another ten minutes of practising trot,

Charlotte's determination to make the most of her ride

started to pay off. She had learnt how to ask Bonnie to

move from trot back to walk by herself and had even improved enough at rising trot to let go with her outside hand. Both Leanne and Helen had praised her a number of times. She was in heaven and it seemed like the ride would never end. But of course it did come to an end.

As Helen told the riders to turn in and follow their leader's instructions to dismount, Charlotte felt tears well up in her eyes. She had loved every second. It was the best time of her life. Not only had she actually ridden a pony, she was the most breathtakingly beautiful and gentle pony Charlotte could imagine. She leaned forward in the saddle, eagerly rubbing Bonnie's neck. She forced herself to smile as enthusiastically as she had done only moment's ago, as Sophie crept into the school and took pictures of her and Bonnie on her phone. Charlotte hoped her friend had managed to get some good photographs. Even though she was upset that it was over, this was certainly a moment that she wished to cherish forever.

ChapterSix

It's all over.

Helen had been kind enough to allow Charlotte and Sophie to lead Bonnie back to her stable. Charlotte knew this would be her only opportunity to thank the pony for the happiness she had just given her and to say good bye. This was it, her long suppressed dream to ride had come true, but now it was over in the blink of an eye. She could never be selfish enough to ask her mum to pay for riding lessons that the family simply couldn't afford. At least Sophie had thought to take a number of photographs and videos on her phone. She would be able to look back on the memories forever.

Charlotte had slid the reins over Bonnie's head and the girls had walked the long way around to the stable yard. Gently, Charlotte coaxed the pony toward her stable block and slid inside with her as Sophie held the door open.

"What do we do with her now?" Charlotte asked sadly.

"We need to tie her reins up in the throat lash and loosen her girth off." Sophie told her.

Charlotte raised her eyebrows, the pony had worked hard for the last hour and they were going to leave her tacked up? It didn't seem fair! Sophie seemed to sense her unease.

"All the ponies are left tacked up if they have another lesson soon after." She explained.

If she wouldn't be riding here again, it wouldn't matter if she got in trouble, Charlotte reasoned to herself. She turned away and fumbled under the saddle flap until she found the girth buckles. They were much tighter than she imagined and it took some time for her to tug them both free and let the girth drop down. All the while, she could sense

Sophie watching her and worrying. Carefully she eased the saddle off, but the girth clattered over the pony's back and startled her for a moment.

"Put the girth over the saddle!" Sophie instructed her, half wanting to not be involved and half wanting to help Charlotte un-tack the pony quickly before they were discovered.

Just the bridle to go Charlotte mused to herself, as she wondered which straps to unfasten. It had seemed so straight forward in the pony magazines, but now with a real life pony here in front of her, it seemed so much more confusing. There were so many straps to the bridle! Charlotte never had the chance to figure it out as both girls heard the sound of feet approaching. Jane! They held their breath. They were in for it now! Even Charlotte, who was normally so confident, so sure of herself, gulped.

Striding around the corner of the stable block appeared Leanne. She stood for a moment, her dark wavy hair blowing around her shoulders as her eyes adjusted to the dim light.

"Just checking you guys are alright in here?" she asked brightly, a friendly smile on her face.

"We umm... we accidentally took Bonnie's saddle off. Charlotte didn't realise the ponies kept them on until it was too late." Sophie stammered, trying to cover for her friend.

"Not to worry. Would you like me to show you how to put it back on?"

Sophie and Charlotte exchanged glances. After the run in with Jane that morning, neither of them had expected Leanne to be so friendly around the stables. Perhaps Jane hadn't told her yet.

"I'm not sure if..."

Before Sophie could finish her sentence, Charlotte cut in, "That'd be great! Thanks!"

With a gentleness that the girls hadn't seen from Jane earlier, Leanne slipped the bottle green saddle pad on to Bonnie's back. As she put the saddle in place, she explained how to ease the saddle pad up into the gullet of the saddle and how to fasten the girth steadily so as not to cause the little pony any discomfort. Next, she unbuckled the throat lash and wound the reins up, before looping the throat lash back through them and buckling it up, explaining that this would help to stop Bonnie getting tangled in her reins whilst she waited for the next lesson. Charlotte was sort of glad that her plan to leave Bonnie un-tacked had failed – she had learnt how to put a saddle on now! Not that it mattered to her.

"Thanks Leanne," she said, "I hope we won't get you in trouble!"

"Why would you get me in trouble?" Leanne asked curiously.

"Oh you know, because Jane doesn't like lesson riders in the stables." Charlotte explained.

Leanne giggled, "I can see why you might think that. Jane just really loves these horses. She doesn't want anyone to do things if they aren't done properly."

Charlotte looked at Sophie and they both shrugged. Jane hadn't seemed like she loved the ponies when she had frightened Sammi earlier. Maybe Leanne just didn't want to say anything bad about her. Not really knowing what to say, Charlotte turned back to Bonnie and held her hand out to her one last time. She sniffed gently and began to nuzzle Charlotte's hand. She tried not to let the tears rise in her eyes as she learnt forward and kissed the roan pony good bye on her velvety muzzle.

"It looks like you're going to have a new friend there," Leanne commented, "See you next week!" She called as she turned to go.

"No!" Charlotte blurted out, "I'm not coming back." She felt the tears begin to rise in her eyes again as her words made the situation so final.

Sensing her discomfort, Sophie began to explain the situation to Leanne. She left out the details about her parents, for which Charlotte was grateful, but explained that the lesson had been a one off early birthday present for Charlotte's up-coming twelfth birthday. When she had finished, Leanne smiled sadly. "What a shame, you were a real natural. It's not so often that lesson riders are so in tune with the ponies like that."

Charlotte smiled weakly. Those kind words had made her feel proud. In a way they were both comforting and a crushing blow. She knew Leanne wasn't just being kind, if she had the opportunity, she could learn to ride really

well. She just knew that she could. But there was no point in delaying what was to come now. She couldn't stay here all day chatting about

ponies. Her own, pony free life was waiting for her to get

back to it. Not daring to spare a backward glance at

Bonnie for fear that she might not be able to leave,

Charlotte linked arms with Sophie and began to walk

back toward the car.

Chapter Seven

Back to reality.

The rest of the weekend had seemed to drag after the adventure at Rockingwood. Charlotte had been glad to be back at school on the Monday. Being so close to the end of the summer term, it had been a hectic few days. The extra netball practises for the final match of the year had been enough to keep Charlotte from thinking too much about how her horsey dream had both become a reality and ended in the course of a morning. Carly Johnson had been promoted to team captain just days earlier and the whole team were training hard to get used to their new captain. Charlotte despised the way Carly treated Sophie and she was certainly much bossier than the old team captain who had moved schools, but Charlotte had to admit that she was by far the best netball player the team had. She was glad of the distraction that the extra netball training had caused. A part of her had been left behind in that stable with Bonnie at the weekend. The thought of the sweet little pony still made her eyes burn.

Today should have been another happy day. It was Charlotte's birthday. Instead of having beans on toast as she usually did on a Wednesday evening with her brothers, Charlotte's mother had arranged to finish work at the taxi firm early, so that the family could enjoy a special birthday tea. She really hoped that her mother had made her a birthday cake. Cake is just the best she thought to herself as she waited by the school bus stop for Sophie. Eventually, Sophie appeared breathlessly from around the corner.

"Sorry, Mr Hordon was late giving out the maths homework." She called to her friend. Sophie was just in time as the bus came into view from down the street. It was only a 20 minute walk home if they missed the bus, but Charlotte wanted to be home as soon as possible.

As the girls settled themselves on to the seats, Sophie pulled a large brown envelope out of her school bag.

"One last birthday present!" she grinned at her best friend.

Charlotte looked curiously at the envelope. What could Sophie have bought her that came in an envelope? Fishing around inside, she thought she could feel glossy paper, adding further to her confusion. Finding an edge to grasp, she pulled the present out of the envelope and gasped. In her hand she held an A4 sized photograph of herself beaming, riding Bonnie in the indoor arena at Rockingwood. Somehow having a printed photograph seemed so much more precious than the digital version. "Thanks Sophie, it's beautiful. I'll treasure it!" She told her friend, and she really meant it.

"Sorry it's not in a frame," Sophie offered, "but mum said she'd look out for one big enough next time she goes to the supermarket."

The two friends chatted easily on the bus ride home. Charlotte had explained that she hadn't had her birthday presents off her mum or brothers yet, but didn't really mind if they hadn't got her anything with money being so tight. She was simply happy to spend extra time with her family. She knew Sophie would understand this and although she had invited Sophie to her birthday tea, she didn't really mind that Sophie hadn't been able to accept the invite.

As Charlotte hopped off the bus, she dashed towards her cottage. Rounding the corner, she saw the curtains twitch as she approached. The front door opened and her mother and brothers popped out, chorusing happy birthday. She grinned, knowing her brothers must have cycled as fast as they could to beat her home from school. Hurrying inside, she was quick to show her mother the thoughtful photograph from Sophie. Despite the heartache horses had given her mother in the past, she had been pretty relaxed about Charlotte's lesson and had offered her some much appreciate comfort when Charlotte had felt sad about leaving Bonnie behind. She had even offered to ask if Charlotte could visit the riding stables occasionally, although Charlotte doubted she would be allowed. Beaming at the photograph, Charlotte mother assured her they would display it in the lounge once a suitable frame had been found.

As they made their way into the small kitchen-dining area, Charlotte noticed her eldest brother, Tom, removing a tea towel that was disguising something on the kitchen table.

"Wow!" she breathed as Tom revealed a birthday cake in the perfect shape of a horse's head. Her mother really was talented at making birthday cakes.

"It's chocolate, your favourite!" Tom told her as he saw her surprise.

"We thought we should indulge your love of horses this year." Her mother explained.

"You don't have to do that." Charlotte protested as her other brother, Luke, groaned even though he was now holding out a rather large gift to her.

Charlotte sat at the kitchen table, secretly thrilled that she did have a present after all. Hurriedly, she began tearing at the colourful wrapping paper, wondering what her brothers had bought her this year. They weren't known for buying the most thoughtful of presents. Discarding the paper on the kitchen table,

Charlotte held up a deep purple hoody. On the front was

the silhouette of a rearing horse. Running the warm

material through her hands, Charlotte caught a glimpse

of gold on the back. Turning it over, she realised her

name was printed in large gold letters across the back.

She laughed, this was possibly the best present her

brothers had ever bought her. Despite the warm

summer afternoon, Charlotte delightedly pulled the

hoody on.

"I take it that means you like it?" Tom teased her.

"I do! Thank you!" Charlotte exclaimed. This wasn't such

a bad birthday after all.

Charlotte opened the pile of cards from her

family and friends as her mother served up her favourite

tea – spaghetti bolognaise.

Although, Charlotte couldn't gulp it down fast enough in her haste to move on to the chocolate horse birthday cake, which would be absolutely delicious. Her mother's cake were always so tasty, she couldn't understand why she didn't sell them. She made a mental note to save a slice for Sophie.

As her mother finally placed a plate down for her with the cake, Charlotte notice a white envelope had been slipped underneath the plate. She had already opened a card from her mother. What could this be? Fishing under the plate, Charlotte pulled out the small envelope. Her name was written on the front in her mother's handwriting. She looked to her mother, but she just grinned back, waiting for her daughter to open the envelope. Much more carefully this time, Charlotte opened the surprise envelope, pulled out a small piece of paper and turned it over. It read:

Charlotte, you have been booked on to not one, but two full pony days at Rockingwood Riding Stables. You will learn how to look after the horses and have a riding lesson on each day.
Happy birthday, love Mum x

Charlotte read and re-read the note. Her mum had done this for her birthday? She couldn't believe it. Surely the hoody had been enough?

"Mum, this is amazing," she stammered, "Surely it's too expensive though, even just for one day?"

"It's your birthday, you're allowed to be spoiled once a year! Besides, when I heard from Sophie's mum about the pony days, I couldn't think of anything better to get you for your birthday. When I phoned on Sunday, Helen explained that you had done so well in your lesson that she offered me a discount on
you doing a second pony day. I couldn't refuse! She even told me she would book one of your lessons on Bonnie. Apparently you made quite an impression!" Her mother explained.

Could this be true? Helen had been *that* pleased with her? Her dream was coming true for the second time in a week. And to ride the magnificent, gentle roan pony again, she simply could not believe it! Saying thank you just didn't seem enough. Rushing forward, Charlotte

embraced her mother in a fierce hug and vowed to

herself that she would help her mother more around the

house over the

 summer to repay her kindness.

The rest of her birthday seemed to pass in a haze.

Further excitement had come when she had text Sophie

to tell her the good news. She had discovered that

Sophie was also booked onto the first of Charlotte's

pony days. Sharing the day with her best friend was the

only way to make it even better! Even though Charlotte

had enjoyed games of tennis and cricket in the garden

with her brothers and even shared an extra slice of cake

with her mother, her mind had been elsewhere. She

thought she might actually burst with

excitement. Two whole weeks she would have to wait until the first pony day. Two weeks! Charlotte had no idea how she would manage to think of anything else except for the little roan pony in that time!

Chapter Eight

Pony Day!

The end of school for the summer holidays had seemed to take an age to arrive after Sophie had learnt the she would be attending the pony day with Charlotte. The girls had talked about nothing else during the final days of school. Mr Hordon had even become so frustrated with Sophie day dreaming about horses during in maths that he had told her she was in need of the summer holidays to pull herself together. Sophie couldn't have agreed more. But she wasn't intending to spend her time thinking about maths. She was going to spend one glorious day with her favourite pony, Sammi. She had already asked Helen, the owner at Rockingwood stables if she could ride him on the pony day. Helen had said she would see what she could do and Sophie was just praying that she had been put down to ride him.

Charlotte and Sophie had everything planned out. They would brush the ponies until they shone and learn to tack up. They would each take photographs on their phones
of the other riding to remind themselves of the day. Afterwards they had planned to sit in the small barn that housed Sammi's and Bonnie's stables to eat their lunch. It was perfect that the two best friends' ponies were tabled next to each other. They had giggled as they had imagined Sammi cheekily trying to steal food from their lunch boxes. Perhaps in the afternoon they would be able to sit in the sunshine polishing the ponies' saddles.

Sophie sighed, today was going to be brilliant. The sun was already shining as they had hoped. If only Charlotte would hurry and get ready! Sophie's mum had dropped her off at

Charlotte's house ten minutes ago and the girls planned

to walk from there to the stables. Sophie had brought a

spare pair of green checked jodhpurs for Charlotte to

borrow. Both girls had the same petite figure so she

knew they would fit. Eventually, Charlotte came dashing

back down the stairs wearing the borrowed jodhpurs

and her new purple horse hoody. They didn't really

match but all Charlotte was interested in was looking as

horsey as possible.

"Come on, let's go!" she declared as if she had been the

one waiting for Sophie.

With a quick call goodbye to her brothers,

Charlotte grabbed Sophie's arm and the two girls dashed

out of the house and down the leafy, green lane towards

Rockingwood stables. As they went, they chatted and giggled about the day ahead.

"Do you think Jane will be ok with us today?" Sophie asked all of a sudden.

"Yeah, why wouldn't she be?" Charlotte questioned, wondering why Sophie always needed to sound so nervous about everything.

"Well it's just that when I went for my lesson at the weekend, she wouldn't let me put
Sammi away. She said we'd caused too much trouble the last time when we un-tacked Bonnie."

Charlotte stopped in her tracks. This was the first she'd heard of this. She'd thought Leanne wouldn't have mentioned the incident to Jane. Once she'd learned that she' be returning to Rockingwood after all, she had even imagined herself making friends with Leanne. She'd seemed so friendly. Now she realised she'd been wrong. Obviously Leanne had betrayed them to Jane and now Jane had taken her anger out on Sophie. Charlotte felt angry too, a black cloud suddenly darkening her perfect day. She knew Sophie wouldn't stand up for herself with this know-it-all Jane. She worried that this could spoil the dream day they had planned. Determined not to let her friend see this, she told her not to worry about it and continued her determined march toward Rockingwood.

They walked for a while in silence before Charlotte said, "We'll just keep out of the way of that know-it-all Jane's." As they rounded the corner and into the driveway of Rockingwood she added, "Let's stick to the plan and go and brush the ponies straight away. Helen will be really pleased when they are so shiny!"

Sophie wasn't sure whether to chuckle at Charlotte's ease of brushing off Jane's comments, or be worried. Nevertheless, they had come to spend a day with the ponies, so they walked straight across the yard to the end barn. It was quiet, with no-one in sight and Sophie supposed they were a little early. They had been eager to get here after all. Once inside the barn, they both dumped their rucksacks in the corner. As Sophie's eyes adjusted to the dim light, she leant over Sammi's stable door and noticed Charlotte was doing the same at Bonnie's door. She could see that Sammi was happily munching away on what must be his breakfast. The delicate black pony stretched out his neck and snorted at her hand, covering it with slime and bits of half eaten feed. Once he realised that Sophie hadn't brought more food, he was instantly disinterested and went back to eating from his breakfast bucket.

"Eeew!" Sophie exclaimed, rubbing her hand clean against her jodhpurs.

Charlotte was already inside Bonnie's stable. Sophie could hear her whispering to the pony, although she couldn't really make out what she was saying. She giggled as she watched Charlotte try to kiss the pony's nose, only for her to turn back to her morning feed.

"Where do you suppose they keep the grooming brushes?" Charlotte asked, looking around.

"I'm not sure, I'm guessing the tack room."

"Well let's nip over and find some. We can't stay in here with nothing to do." Charlotte replied confidently.

As they crossed the cobbled yard, Sophie could make out a figure in the tack room. Hopefully it would be Helen putting up the list of rides for the day. Drawing nearer, Sophie realised it was Leanne. She hoped Charlotte wouldn't go saying anything to her. Her friend could be so feisty at times and often didn't think before she spoke when she was annoyed.

"Morning you two. Are you looking forward to the pony day?" she asked, once again turning her smiling face towards them.

"Um yeah, we can't wait to brush the ponies!" Sophie told her. Charlotte just glared and said nothing.

"Well you can pop your rucksacks in this box, that's where everyone puts them and then we can get started." Leanne explained.

Sophie felt relieved that Leanne was being so friendly. Perhaps today was getting off to a good start. As they retrieved their bags from the barn, Jane strode into the tack room,

stopping right in the doorway. The sun glaring behind her made her look more imposing than usual, as Sophie squinted from

the dim light of the tack room. Without so much as a good morning, Jane began, "There's still a few pony day children to arrive so you two can be making a start. Stables one to five need mucking out. Leanne will show you how to do the first one, then it's down to you two."

Sophie hadn't given any thought to mucking out. She wasn't sure what to say next. All of a sudden, Charlotte started to speak, "Mucking out? Shouldn't we be brushing the ponies to get them ready?" She blurted out, staring straight at Jane.

In response, Jane merely snorted a sort of laugh, turned on her heal and left.

Sophie and Charlotte looked at each other. This wasn't what they had planned!

"It's the first job we do every day," Leanne offered as they followed her to collect mucking out tools, "it's an important part of looking after the horses."

Sophie knew she was right. She was sure there would be plenty of time for grooming and riding later in the day. Charlotte was oddly silent as Leanne led them to the first empty stable and began to explain how to muck out the straw bed. She showed them how to toss

the straw to find any dirty bedding and pointed out

where they would need to go to change the horse's

water bucket.

"I think you can probably manage this by yourselves, I'll

pop back in ten minutes to check you're ok." Leanne told

them.

This is where Charlotte, who had been quietly seething,

jumped in. "What are you checking up on us for? So you

can report back to Jane that we messed up and get us in

trouble again?" She snapped.

Leanne looked shocked at Charlotte's harsh words,

"What are you talking about? Why

would I do that?" she asked, suddenly looking very

young.

"You were quick to get us in trouble when I took Bonnie's saddle off. Jane couldn't wait to be mean to Sophie!"

"I didn't...wait, I had to explain to Jane what took me so long but I didn't mean to get you in trouble...sorry if I did Sophie." Leanne said with more kindness than they deserved after Charlotte's outburst.

Sophie could see that Charlotte looked unwilling to accept the apology and stepped in, "Thanks Leanne...we're sorry. We know it wasn't your fault really." She offered.

"That's ok, I know what it's like to be on Jane's bad side too." With that she smiled and left the two friends to their mucking out.

It took slightly over an hour for the girls to muck the stables out. Sophie had been eager to do as neat a job as possible to try and make it up to Leanne. She had popped back a couple of times and said Jane would be pleased with their work. Even though neither girl was fond of Jane, knowing she would like their work pleased them. After all, she was talented and experienced with the horses. By the time they had finished, Sophie couldn't stop sneezing.

"Eugh! Hay fever!" She declared, rubbing at her nose and eyes with her sleeve.

"Let's take these tools back and get a drink."

As they made their way into the tack room, there was a small gathering of children surrounding Helen, the owner of, and instructor at Rockingwood Riding Stables.

"There you are! Jane told me that you too were keen to help with the mucking out. You're just in time, we're deciding what is going to happen today." Helen explained. Sophie barely had the chance to wonder why Jane had told her they were eager to muck out, as Helen explained the day would start with a demonstration in grooming and tacking up. After that, the less experienced riders would have a lesson whilst those with more experience could choose between a lesson and a hack out. At the end of the day there was going to be a gymkhana for everyone. A gymkhana, Sophie thought excitedly! She was thrilled. She had read about these in her magazines with Charlotte but had never actually thought she'd be lucky enough to take part in one!

"Well?" Charlotte was saying, staring at her.

"Huh?" Was Sophie's only response. She was so busy thinking about the gymkhana that she'd no idea what

Charlotte had said to her.

"Are you going on a hack out or having a lesson?"
Charlotte asked again, sounding a little annoyed.

Sophie considered the choices. She had a lesson every
week. It was rare they went out for a hack, only on the
very hottest of days. She could just imagine Sammi
galloping up the hill behind the stables, his black mane
blowing in the breeze.

"I think I'll go for a hack." She said after a moment,
grinning.

Chapter Nine

Riding!

Before any of them rode, Jane had explained what each of the different grooming brushes were used for and had demonstrated how to use them on the quiet coloured pony, Eddie. Sophie was surprised at how patient Jane had been in her explanations. Perhaps she wasn't as bad as they thought. Once she was satisfied that everyone knew what to use each brush for, they had been allowed to work in pairs to brush a pony under Jane's supervision. Sammi and Bonnie had both been tied up in the yard. Sophie could see that

Charlotte was seething as another pair had been allocated Bonnie to brush. Her friend was clearly itching to go over to her favourite pony. On the other hand,

Sophie was thrilled, this was her chance to make Sammi shine!

As they finished off grooming Sammi, Sophie's thrill came to an abrupt end. Helen came over to give her some bad news that would burst her bubble, as she told her that she would be riding Rosie on the hack and not Sammi. Seeing the look of disappointment on Sophie's face, she was quick to explain that she never let anyone hack out on Sammi, except for on the lead rode. In the past when he'd thought he was going for a canter, he'd bucked dangerously and bolted off into a gallop. Remembering the brief horror she'd felt when Sammi had bolted in her lesson just a couple of weeks ago, Sophie suddenly felt relieved, although tried not to show it.

Within minutes, the yard became a flurry of activity. Charlotte and another girl had gone off with Helen to learn how to tack

 up Bonnie and Eddie. Sophie had gone with Leanne to tack up Rosie. The dun pony had mostly ignored them as they'd gotten her ready, preferring instead to tug at her haynet in the front corner of her stable. Leanne had shown Sophie how to fit the bridle correctly, before removing it and letting Sophie try for herself. She was pleased that she'd done it easily, with only a little reminder from Leanne about fastening the nose band.

Despite not being mounted on her favourite pony, Sophie felt content as the ride began to make its way out of the ride at

Rockingwood. As well as her, there was Jake riding the chestnut thoroughbred, Penny, in front of her and Jane at the front of the ride on the ironically named Tiny, a 16.2hh dark bay cob mare. Charlotte would be having a lesson in the school whilst she was out.

Sophie soon settled into the stride of the dun mare. At 14.2hh, she was a little bigger than she was used to with Sammi and certainly much wider! But the mare had an easy way about her. The ride made its way out of the driveway and along the road to the bridleway. Luckily, there was a particularly wide grass verge which ran the length of the road so the riders had no need to actually be on the road with the cars. Sophie was grateful, the thought made her shudder. Jane signalled for the ride to move into a trot. Rosie was surprisingly easy to hold back, even when Jake had moved off in front of her. The pony had a much longer stride than Sammi, giving her a much smoother trot. Sophie was starting to enjoy herself. Eventually they came to the far end of the road and dropped back into a walk. Looking back over her shoulder, Sophie could just make out the buildings at Rockingwood in the distance. In front of her, Penny was pawing at the grass impatiently as the riders stood waiting for Jane to open the gate onto the bridleway.

"Are you ok?" Sophie called to Jake as the horse seemed to become more agitated.

"Yeah, she's just getting a bit..."

Before he could finish Jane cut in, "Give her a smack on the neck before she cuts all the grass up."

Sophie thought it a little harsh to be giving the horse a smack but supposed Jane had a point about the grass. Jake did as he was told and gave the mare a light tap on her neck with his crop. Penny snorted and backed up at the unexpected shock. Sophie felt a slight panic as the horse flashed it's ears back and continued to back towards her. Just in time, Jane managed to open the gate. Penny shot past, through the narrow gateway, narrowly avoiding knocking Jake's legs against the fence post. Phew! She was glad not to have been given Penny to ride, she looked mad! Rosie went forwards much more easily and once everyone was through the gate they began to trot up the hill on the path which would lead them past the old windmill. Trotting seemed to settle Penny down but Sophie decided to keep Rosie back a little, just in case.

As the hill became a little steeper, Sophie leaned forward slightly in the saddle as she rose to the trot, knowing this would make it a little easier for the pony.

As they reached the old windmill Jane signaled for them to drop back into walk. Sophie knew that once they passed the derelict stone building, whose sails had long since stop spinning, the track would start to drop away downhill. It would be much safer at a walk. Rosie picked her way easily downwards, even when the track was a little bumpy and rocky. This was the first time Sophie had ever hacked out on Rosie and watching as Penny spooked to the side at a passing pheasant, she knew she felt safe.

Once down the hill, the group turned back in the direction of Rockingwood along a winding, narrow, wooded path. A number of times, Sophie had to duck down against Rosie's warm next to avoid low hanging branches. She gave the pony a comforting pat on her neck and tousled her mane as she continued to pick her way forward through the trees. Sophie breathed in the smell of the trees and what seemed to be the smell of wild garlic growing. This really was heaven, even though the sun wasn't making its way through

the trees and she felt a chill. Blissfully, it seemed to take an age to reach the far end of the woodland path.

"We're going to turn right, head over the bridge and canter up the stubble field," Jane called over her shoulder, "Is everyone OK with that?"

"Yeah, Penny's a bit excited though!" Jake called cheerfully.

"Sophie?"

"Sounds good, Rosie is pretty settled." She called from the back.

Crossing the small stone bridge over the trickling stream, Rosie held her breath. Even though nothing had ever happened, she could just imagine toppling over the edge and falling into the stream. It was silly, but it worried her all the same. Up ahead, Penny, who seemed to know she was going for a canter was jumping about from side to side and snorting. Sophie saw Jane turn around to give Jake instructions, but nothing seemed to calm the horse.

Emerging from a clearing and into the sunlight, the riders entered the stubble field. There was a wide grass path that ran the length of the field, although today there were no crops within the field to worry about, the
farmer had already harvested them. With no warning, Penny suddenly leapt up into the air and surged forward at a mad gallop, quickly passing Jane and Tiny who had set off at a steady canter.

Sophie felt butterflies in her stomach as she hoped Rosie wouldn't follow. Luckily, the mare listened carefully to Rosie's instructions to canter. She went forward at some speed but didn't pull at the reins as Sammi had done in the school. In fact, Rosie seemed to have a gentle, soft mouth. She didn't pull at all. Her thick black mane flew up at her in the wind as

they thudded along the grass. Up ahead, she could see Jane pushing Tiny forwards, trying to keep up with Penny to shout instructions to Jake, to help slow down the excitable thoroughbred. Sophie whooped and soon lost herself in the thrill of the moment. She didn't see the pheasant in the hedgerow. In an instant, it flew up, nearly brushing against poor Rosie's face.

Rosie swerved jerkily to the left, startled. Sophie clung on with all her might, trying desperately not to be thrown from the side of the spooking pony. The saddle began to slide down the right hand side of Rosie's wide belly. Sophie didn't know what to do. She was using all of her strength to prevent herself from sliding right off. Gritting her teeth, she managed to find a final bit of energy and pulled awkwardly on the reins. It was a miracle that Rosie came to a standstill. She seemed confused as to why her rider was hanging halfway down her side and didn't move any further, despite her fright.

Sophie grasped hold of a handful of mane with her hand. She tried to right herself and leaned toward the horse trying to pull herself upward.

It was not use. She was simply too far down the side.

What should she do? Hold on tight and hope to be

rescued? Try to dismount? She worried that if she tried

to dismount, her foot would become stuck in the stirrup

and cause her to fall dangerously underneath Rosie.

Clinging on and trying not to panic, she could hear cries

from further down the track. She couldn't tell whether it

was for her or perhaps whether Jake had had an

accident on the madly galloping horse.

Relief flooded through her as Jane quickly came

alongside her. She'd approached sensibly, walking on

foot so as not to startle Rosie and cause her to spook.

Moving around to the opposite side from where Sophie

was dangling, she grasped the cantle of the saddle and

heaved with all her might to right the stricken rider.

When Sophie was far enough up, she used her weight in the stirrup to help straighten the saddle.

"Didn't you tighten the girth?" Jane snapped, "You're lucky you didn't fall off!"

"I thought it was OK," Sophie mumbled, "Leanne did it up. She spooked at a pheasant." She was close to tears now from the shock.

The last thing she needed was a telling off as well.

By now Jake had come up alongside them, riding a still excitable Penny whilst leading Tiny alongside.

"Crikey Sophie, that was amazing staying on like that!" Jake enthused in his easy going manner.

"I guess the girth is tight enough after all," Jane offered after she finished inspecting it. "Just try and stay sat in the middle, it doesn't help that Rosie's so fat!" she finished as she made her way back over to Tiny. "If everyone is OK, we'll take it steady on the ride back.

It took about 15 minutes to work their way back up the cobbled path towards the stables. Even Penny seemed to settle down as the riders picked their way steadily home. Sophie's nerves had calmed down too by the time they clattered back into the stable yard. As Sophie swung down from the saddle, Charlotte came dashing over to meet her, a grin plastered on her face.

"You'll never guess what?" her friend cried breathlessly. Sophie looked at her and tried to put the ride behind her and look cheerful for her friend, "What?"

"I rode Bonnie off the lead rope. We walked and trotted, I even managed a figure of eight in trot! Can you believe it? "

Sophie couldn't believe it. It was practically unheard of for someone to do so well on only their second ride. She wasn't surprised, Charlotte was so enthusiastic and determined. Her friend could do anything she put her mind to. With that, Sophie cheered up as the girls chatted excitedly and set about helping to put the ponies away.

Chapter Ten

Gymkhana!

The girls had been so busy helping to fill hay nets that they had been too late to have lunch in the tack room with the other pony day children. Not that they minded, they would have much rather sat with Sammi and Bonnie! Instead, they sat amongst the hay in the hay barn eating their sandwiches with Leanne and Jake. Leanne had explained that they weren't allowed to have their lunch in the little stable block that housed Bonnie and Sammi. The girls understood when Leanne had explained that the ponies would get too excited and think the food was for them. The hay tickled at Sophie's nose but she didn't mind too much.

Charlotte, who was much more at ease with new people than Sophie, had chatted easily with the others and peppered them with questions. They had found out that Leanne was in fact only a year older than them, but didn't go to their school. She had been helping out at Rockingwood for almost a year. Jake had been helping out for much longer and was allowed to ride any of the horses. He was fourteen and explained that he hoped to get enough experience to be able to go and work in an eventing yard when he was older.

Jake had a pleasant manner about him and Sophie knew he wasn't being unkind when he told the others about the eventful ride out, even though Sophie had hoped the ground would swallow her whole.

"What, I can't believe you didn't tell me about this!"

Charlotte cried. "That's amazing Sophie, you're such a good rider staying on like that!"

"Yeah she did great clinging on like that. It was impossible!" Jake chipped in politely.

The truth was Sophie hadn't wanted to say anything and cause a fuss. She still felt uneasy about the way Jane had blamed her.

"Thanks," she managed, "I don't think Jane was very pleased though."

Charlotte had pressed Sophie to tell her what had happened with Jane. Sophie already knew that her friend was taking a disliking to the head groom and this incident had just added to her feelings. If Charlotte was going to come to the stables again, she didn't want Jane to not like her.

"She's such a know-it-all!" Charlotte exclaimed. This seemed to be one of her favourite sayings.

"It's just her job to make sure everything is done properly to keep everyone safe." Jake offered, trying not to get dragged into Charlotte's obvious dislike for Jane.

"Hmmm." Charlotte replied, clearly not satisfied.

"Perhaps if you're going to be coming to the stables more often you'll start to like her." Leanne offered.

"I won't be coming to the stables after the next pony day. They were birthday presents. Mum can't afford lessons." Charlotte explained grumpily.

"Why don't you offer to come and help out then?" Leanne suggested, "We come most days in the holidays and get a lesson every week. We still come at weekends during term time and Helen normally gives us a lesson at the end of the month."

This sparked a thought in Charlotte's mind. She hadn't thought about helping out before and especially hadn't considered that she might get rides in return. It seemed like a wonderful idea. The best! But would she be allowed? Sophie had told her in the past that she'd love to help out at the stables but didn't dare ask because she didn't think she'd be

good enough. Then again, Sophie was always such a worrier, mused Charlotte. As the children packed away their lunch bags and set about getting the ponies ready for the gymkhana, Charlotte's mind was working overtime on the idea.

By mid afternoon, the gymkhana games had been set up in the large outdoor school. All of the riders were gathered around Helen, who was explaining each of the activities. There would be a bending race, flag race, egg

and spoon race and an around the world where riders

would take their feet out of their

 stirrups and turn all the way around on their ponies.

Everyone was ready and an electric atmosphere filled

the air. Jake was mounted on Rosie, Eva was riding an

11.2hh chestnut gelding named Casper and Jenny was

on Poppy, a 13hh bay mare. Jake had explained he was

competing in the gymkhana to get some experience for a

show in the summer holidays. Sophie was mounted on

her beloved Sammi and Charlotte was on Bonnie. She

had been allowed to sit on Bonnie and wait without a

leader and hoped she would be allowed to complete the

races off the lead rein too, she was sure she was up to it!

The riders began to line up in their lanes.

Charlotte kicked Bonnie forward into a walk. She knew

the way she used her reins to turn her was hardly neat and tidy but she managed to get her across to the end lane. She hoped this was it, they were ready to start and she didn't need a leader! It was only when she turned and looked behind her that she saw Jane striding toward her holding a lead rope. She sighed. Of all the people that had to lead her, it had to be Jane! The way she treated people made Charlotte so angry.

After clipping on the lead rope, Jane gave Charlotte the briefest of smiles.

"Do you know what you need to do for the bending race?" she asked.

"Yes," was Charlotte's only reply, in a tone that clearly indicated she didn't want to discuss it any further. Did Jane think she was stupid? Of course she understood the rules. Perhaps she could accidentally kick her while she was leading her, Charlotte thought. That would show her.

On the blow of Helen's whistle, the riders all urged their ponies forwards. Jake and Rosie surged forward ahead of the other riders. Charlotte gritted her teeth and kicked

Bonnie into a faster trot. She tightly gripped the front of the saddle with both hands to help her keep her balance. She hadn't trotted this fast before! Bonnie seemed eager, her little ears pricked as they approached the first bending pole. Panic suddenly gripped Charlotte. How would she turn her whilst holding onto the saddle? If she let go to turn, she might bounce right off. Before she could decide, Jane turned the pony around the bending pole. Phew, Charlotte felt relieved, Jane was actually helping her. As they made their way through the bending poles, she could see Jake already turning at the far end of the arena to make his way back to the finish. The dun pony was flying! No-one would beat them now. Sophie looked like she had her hands full as Sammi was pulling at the bit, trying to go faster. She was neck and neck with Jenny and Poppy. Only Eva and little Casper were slightly ahead of her. There didn't seem to be any more she could do to catch on the others, but it didn't really matter. In no time at all, they'd wound their way back down the arena, bending around the poles as they went. Charlotte hadn't dared let go of the saddle to turn, although she had managed to get Bonnie to trot a little faster, causing Jane to break into a jog as she led them.

As they came to a stop at the finishing line, Charlotte was exhausted. The race had been great fun!

"You'll have to go faster than that if you don't want to lose every race." Jane told her scornfully as they turned to line up for the next race.

Charlotte gawped at her. "It doesn't matter about winning. Everyone is having fun. Except you." Charlotte snapped at her, trying to sound firm. How dare she be so rude! Maybe she would go faster. So fast that stupid Jane
 wouldn't be able to keep up with them. That'd do it. She'd worked out now how to get Bonnie to trot faster. We can do it girl, she thought to herself as she leant forward to give the pony an encouraging rub on her neck.

Despite her determination, Charlotte couldn't do it though. Concentrating to hold the egg and spoon and flag whilst she was trotting was a big enough challenge in itself. She had managed to come fourth in the egg and spoon race as Jenny had dropped her egg twice, meaning Charlotte could overtake as she dismounted. In the flag race she had

managed to accidentally on purpose poke Jane with the flag, although she wasn't sure she had really noticed. Now there was only one race left to show Jane that she wasn't some dumb kid who she could treat like an idiot.

When the whistle blew for the final race, Charlotte was ready. She used all her strength to send Bonnie forward as fast as she could. The little roan pony was excited now and surged forward. This was it. They flew towards the far end of the arena. Bonnie's mane flew up in the wind. They were trotting at such a pace, Jane had practically broken into a sprint to keep up with them. Charlotte grinned madly. Jane wouldn't be telling her how slow she was again. She still clung to the saddle to help her rise to the fast trot, but she was confident now. Only Jake and Sophie reached the far end of the arena before them and began their 'around the world.' Leanne met them as Bonnie pulled to a halt. She helped Charlotte through the round the world movement. As she turned to sit backward, she glanced across to see Sophie was also in the backward position on Sammi, only he had tucked his head between his knees and was giving almighty bucks. Helen dashed towards him and grabbed hold of his bridle. Charlotte briefly worried about her friend, but if she was going to do well, there was no time to dwell. With Leanne's help, she swung her leg round to face sideways and then back forwards again. Before they set off, Jane thrust the lead rope into Leanne's hand. There was only Jake in front of her again. She urged Bonnie on to the speed she'd gone before. Leanne ran easily beside them as they made their way toward the finish. Second! They'd come second! Charlotte could hardly contain herself. Leanne beamed at her as she leant over to catch her breath.

"Well done Charlotte!" Sophie called to her as she made it over the finish line in fourth place, having survived the bucking.

"I didn't think you had it in you to go that fast yet." Jake told her good naturedly.

As they began to lead their ponies out of the school, Charlotte was gushing. She'd expected to come last in every gymkhana game. In fact being such an inexperienced rider, she'd not even known if she'd be able to do them at all. Now Jake and Leanne had praised her. Even Helen had told her she'd done well. Surely not even Jane could be disappointed after she'd managed to go so much faster. If she was going to ask at becoming a helper at Rockingwood, perhaps now would be a good time to ask. Surely they would see how desperate she was to learn and how much she loved riding. She would ask for Sophie too, she knew her friend would never pluck up the courage to, despite the fact that it was something she dreamed about.

Quickly crossing to the yard, Charlotte saw Helen in the tack room and hurried across. Jane was in there too but she knew this wasn't the time to be worrying about her. She'd have to bite the bullet.

"Hi," she started more awkwardly than she'd have liked, "I was just wondering if I could talk to you about..."

She was abruptly cut off by the sound of Helen's phone.

"Sorry Charlotte, it's the farrier." Helen told her apologetically as she dashed away.

Charlotte's heart sank. She'd built herself up to the moment. Before she could leave, Jane cut in, "What do you want?"

There was an uncomfortable silence for a moment as Charlotte decided whether to ask Jane.

"Well the thing is, I was thinking that maybe I could..." Before she could say the words, Jane cut her off, a smirk creasing her lips.

"Maybe what you could do, is think about the safety of your pony before you go charging around like you've been around horses all your life. You kids, you're all the same, only interested in riding."

With that outburst, Jane turned on her heel and stormed across the yard. Charlotte was speechless. What was she talking about? She loved Bonnie. She hadn't put her in danger, surely? She was so taken back by the unexpected dressing down, that she sat herself down to compose herself before it was time to meet Sophie for the walk home. No wonder Sophie was too nervous to ask to come and help out. Charlotte didn't know what to do now. If Helen felt the same way, there was no way they'd be allowed to help out. She could have spoilt both of their chances. Perhaps going so fast really was selfish and stupid. Something told her though that had Helen been cross with her, she would have said something by now. The problem was Jane's, she was almost sure of that.

As she collected her bag, the one thing she was positive

of was the next time she was at Rockingwood, she would

show Jane that she couldn't treat her that way. She just

had to think of something.

Chapter Eleven

Revenge

Charlotte had arrived at the yard early on the day of her final pony day. Her mum had offered to drop her off, but she'd cycled the short distance instead to get her thoughts together. She'd realised she couldn't do anything drastic to Jane. However, she did have a plan to embarrass her, just as she'd embarrassed Charlotte. She had decided it wouldn't be fair to include Sophie in her plans, so had set her plan for revenge in motion by herself, a few nights ago. Other than revenge, her plan was simple; impress Helen so much that she couldn't turn down her offer of help at Rockingwood.

As soon as she had arrived, she had headed straight for the mucking out tools instead of waiting in the tack room where all of the other pony day children would be waiting for the day to start. Using her initiative, Charlotte had located two empty stables and began mucking out. It wasn't until she had finished the second stable and was pushing the wheel barrow toward the muck heap that she saw Helen and Jane striding back toward the yard from the direction of the fields. Jane never spoke to her. Instead, she just stood there with a frown on her face. Quite the opposite, Helen was beaming at her.

"How nice to see you again Charlotte. It looks like you've been busy already."

"I wanted to do something useful." She told her enthusiastically.

"Well thank you, you've certainly done that," Helen grinned, "Come and join us in the tack room as soon as you've finished."

The frosty greeting from Jane didn't matter, Helen was pleased with her already and that was all that counted. Charlotte smiled happily to herself. This part of her plan was going well already. Hurriedly, she put the mucking out tools away in the barn and headed to the tack room. There were quite a few other children there for the pony day now. Looking around, she noticed Jake was sat to one side and crossed to sit next to him. Leanne would no doubt be around somewhere too. It was odd not being at the stables with Sophie. Although her friend had her weekly lesson booked for that afternoon, it still meant Charlotte would spend the day without her. Charlotte wasn't too worried, she made new friends quite easily. At least Jake was a familiar face too. He gave her his usual friendly greeting. Charlotte smiled back. She felt that they had really started to get to know him and Leanne the last time they were here.

As Helen gave them their morning briefing, she explained that Jake would be helping them this morning but would be busy with gymkhana practise from lunch time. That meant that all of the pony day riders would be riding in the indoor school and there would be no hacks out. There were a few moans from around the room but Charlotte didn't mind, she wasn't experienced enough to be hacking out anyway. She was just a little disappointed that Jake wouldn't be around in the afternoon. The next piece of news Helen shared made Charlotte's heart sink further. Leanne wouldn't be at the yard today to help out the riders. Her mother had phoned to say she was sick. With Jake busy and Leanne sick, Charlotte would just have to hope she got along well with some of the other children on the pony day. Jane certainly wouldn't be keeping her company.

Charlotte was told that she was paired up with a more experienced girl named Carly, who wasn't in the tack room as she had only just started mucking out a stable. Charlotte crossed the yard and found her with her back to the open door. Charlotte thought she could make out Carly texting on her phone. Carly had her long blonde hair in a neat plait and wore a pristine pair of beige jodhpurs, teamed with a matching shiny black pair of long, leather boots. Her whole appearance was in sharp contrast to Charlotte's who still wore the borrowed, green checked jodhpurs from Sophie and who's own blonde hair was in a messy pony tail.

"Hi," Charlotte called out cheerfully, keen to make a good impression. The smile on her face froze on her face as the girl turned around. Carly Johnson! She couldn't quite believe it! She had never known that Carly even liked horses. The last place she had ever expected to find the netball captain, was mucking out the stables. Somehow she still looked immaculate. Charlotte wasn't really surprised at that.

"Charlotte?" Carly said, looking as shocked as Charlotte had only a moment ago.

For a moment, an awkward silence filled the air. Charlotte was well aware of how Carly had taunted Sophie. She'd heard her calling her horse face. To find her here of all places was the last thing Charlotte would ever have expected. "What are you doing here?" she asked curiously, trying to keep the sudden feeling of hostility out of her voice. As Charlotte set about mucking out the stables, she found Carly to be quite chatty, which was a relief really. Although, she did notice that Carly did absolutely nothing to help her to muck out and preferred to watch Charlotte do all of the hard work. Carly had breezily told her that she had ridden since she was small, but had spent her time riding some 'proper' ponies belonging to her parent's friends, just down the road from Rockinwood. Charlotte wasn't sure what she meant by 'proper' ponies, but was sure this was Carly's way of putting her down.

Carly had actually only started riding at Rockingwood recently. Her parents had decided that if she completed a course of pony days over the spring, they would start looking for her a horse of her own over the summer holidays. Carly had complained that she didn't really need to be on the pony days as she already knew how to look after horses, but she'd gone along with her parents wishes anyway. She'd excitedly told her how they had already got some top jumping horse lined up to view the following week. Whilst Charlotte had thought that Carly was a little over bearing, she had decided that she actually seemed very knowledgeable about horses. She must be if she was getting her own horse. She just couldn't figure out why she'd never heard about how much she liked horses before. She couldn't understand why she and Sophie weren't friends. They had so much in common. With

151

Leanne not here, Charlotte had decided to stick with Carly for the day, she was obviously someone who she could learn a lot from. She could put up with listening to Carly going on and on about getting her own horse if it meant learning more to impress Helen.

As soon as they had finished their tasks, the girls headed back to the tack room to find out who they would be riding. Carly had hoped to be riding Penny. She'd said that Penny was the only horse at Rockingwood worth doing any jumping on. Charlotte couldn't understand why she was being so harsh. All of the horses at Rockingwood seemed amazing to her. As they looked at the tack room board, Charlotte could tell that Carly was pleased to see that she had been allocated Penny for the morning lesson.

There would be two lessons in the morning for the pony day riders, one for the more advanced riders and one for those still learning. Charlotte scanned the list, desperate to see her name next to Bonnie's, but she couldn't find her name at all. Had she been missed off? Perhaps she should go and find Helen to ask.

Cautiously, she crossed the cobbled yard towards the house Helen shared with her
 husband, hoping no-one would mind her knocking on the door. Before she could reach it, Helen appeared. She didn't look as composed as she normally did.
"Ah Charlotte, just the person." Helen called as she caught sight of her.

Charlotte looked confused. Helen had spoken in a voice that sounded like she was about to deliver bad news.

Why was she even looking for her? Trying not to panic, she crossed to where Helen now stood waiting for her. "Jane has told me that Bonnie is a little bit stiff this morning. It's probably because she did an extra lesson yesterday. She is fifteen years old

 after all. So I'm afraid that means you won't be able to ride her today. I'm sure she'll be ok in a day or so." Helen explained.

"Oh," Charlotte didn't know what to say, "Is that why I'm not on the list to ride?" she asked, trying to keep the sadness out of her voice.

Helen laughed, the black cloud that had surrounded her only moments before seemed to lift, "No of course not. I know how much these two days mean to you and you've really impressed me with how quickly you've learnt to ride so far.

I thought I'd give you a private lesson on the lunge."

"Really, you'd do that? I don't know what to say!"
Charlotte beamed.

"You've earned it after this morning anyway."

"Thank you Helen, that's amazing. I'll ride anyone, I
don't mind." Charlotte offered. She half meant it. Of
course she'd had her heart set on riding Bonnie, but if
she wasn't up to it and she was getting a private lesson,
she didn't mind.

"You can ride Poppy. It just means you'll have to occupy
yourself around the yard until the other lessons are
finished." Helen explained, a smile spreading across her
face.

"Oh I can do that!" Charlotte enthused. Before she could
be stopped, she turned and dashed at a brisk walk
toward Bonnie's stable. She might not be able to ride her

but she could go and give her some extra attention to cheer her up a bit.

Drawing back the bolt, Charlotte slid into Bonnie's stable. Bonnie turned to look at her. The white blaze down her face had pieces of hay stuck to it. "Here girl," Charlotte cooed at her, gently brushing the hay away with her hand. She wondered whether the little pony was beginning to recognise her. Charlotte's heart sank as the pony turned toward her. It was obvious that she was moving awkwardly, making much smaller, shuffled steps. Tears welled in her eyes, seeing the pony in such discomfort and she fought hard not to let the tears drop. She stepped forward so as the little roan pony didn't have to move any further and buried her face in her long, greyish-pink mane.

Charlotte wrapped her arms around the pony's neck and stroked her kindly. In return, Bonnie gently nuzzled her back. She had only known her for a few days, but she loved her already. The thought of Bonnie being in pain was almost too much to bear. It seemed like an age that they stood there, girl and pony comforting each other. It was only when Carly appeared in the doorway of the small barn, that Charlotte realised how long she had been there.

Taking a moment to collect herself, Charlotte took a deep breath and headed out into the yard. She'd been paired with Carly again to help get the horses ready for the

more advanced lesson. Carly was already re-appearing from the tack room with a saddle and bridle and heading toward Penny's stable. Charlotte sighed. That was the last horse she wanted to go in with, she remembered how Penny had flashed her ears back and bared her teeth on her first day at Rockingwood. She hoped that Penny wouldn't make her look like a wimp in front of Carly. She'd never live it down at school if she did. Still she supposed she'd best go and help.

"Did you tell Helen you weren't down for the lesson?" Carly asked cheerfully as Charlotte slipped into the stable behind her.

"Umm yeah, she said she's decided to give me a private lunge lesson instead."

"What?" Carly snapped, "You've only been here two minutes. Why would she want to give you a private lesson?" Her tone had changed now. Charlotte didn't think she sounded so friendly any more.

"I don't know. I didn't ask her to," Charlotte told her, trying to salvage the situation, "Do you want me to hold her while you put the saddle on?" She offered.

"Yeah. Watch it though. She might bite you." Carly sniped and turned her back on her.

She didn't let the encounter with Carly upset her. After all, she doubted she would see her again for a while after today. She was probably only jealous of her private lesson. She seemed like the jealous type at school, Charlotte thought as she remembered how Carly had once told another girl how awful her netball skirt looked, yet had turned up to the next practise in the exact same one. Anyway, Charlotte had much more important things to think about. For the next hour, Charlotte dashed around the yard grooming ponies for the lessons and where she could, helped to tack up for the lessons.

Only once the novice lesson was underway and the more experienced riders were un-tacking their horses, did Charlotte find herself getting a break in the tack room. Jane was there too, having a drink of tea. This was her perfect opportunity. Pulling her rucksack from the corner, Charlotte fished around and pulled out a bag of sweets. She pulled out her favourite strawberry chew, before turning to Jane.

"Do you want a sweet?" She asked, trying to keep her voice calm and friendly, as she held the bag out toward her. Jane looked at her suspiciously, as if no one had ever offered her a sweet before. Charlotte mused that they probably hadn't if she was always so rude to people.

"Thanks," Jane mumbled, after what seemed like an age. Charlotte noticed how she actually took a handful of sweets. Typical. Jane settled herself back down with her tea and sweets and began to flick through a horse magazine. Without waiting any longer, Charlotte coolly placed the bag away and headed out of the tack room. The yard was just filling up with

 the advanced riders leading their horses away for untacking. Everyone was busy. This was her chance.

　　　Turning away from the stables, Charlotte crept through the barn toward the muck heap. The main muck heap was out of sight around the back of the indoor school. Day to day, the helpers used the small wooden muck trailer that was attached to the back of a small tractor. You had to push your wheelbarrow up a narrow wooden plank into the back of the trailer. Charlotte took

a deep breath and looked around to check that no one

could see her. She'd be in for it if they did.

The coast was clear. Silently, Charlotte slipped a

screw driver out of her hoodie pocket. She had sneakily

slipped it in there when she had taken the sweets out of

her rucksack. The screw driver actually belonged to her

brother, but she was sure he wouldn't notice it was

missing for one day. Before she could talk herself out of

it, Charlotte quickly loosened off the screws that held

the wooden plank to the back of the muck trailer. She

was careful not to let the screws fall to the floor. She

didn't want them to make a noise and draw attention to

her. Only once all of the screws were loose did she pull

them all free and place them on the floor as if they had

just fallen out. For a final touch, Charlotte slid the ramp

a little to be sure that it would fall when Jane walked up it.

This was going to be brilliant! Charlotte had to try hard not to laugh out loud at the thought of the ramp collapsing and covering Jane in manure! She didn't want to hang around the trailer and give the game away, so she stealthily slipped away and began filling hay nets. It was just the job. She would look busy, but from the hay barn she would have a great view of the muck trailer to see what would happen.

It didn't take her long to find out. In less than two minutes, she saw Jane amble down the yard with a wheelbarrow. She had been skipping out the stables ready for lunch time. Charlotte made a point of not watching as Jane headed toward the trailer, so as not to look suspicious. At the last moment, Charlotte looked around to see Jane dashing up the plank. As she was half way up, the plank slip free of the trailer and crashed to the ground.

Charlotte's eyes widened and she gasped at the sight. Jane's wheelbarrow flew off the ramp, partly covering Jane with the
smelly contents. Oh what a glorious moment! It didn't completely cover her, but it was enough to make tears of laughter well up in Charlotte's eyes. Her plan for revenge had worked brilliantly! As the others heard the commotion and began to dash toward Jane, Charlotte could barely contain herself. She hadn't expected that so many people would be around to see. She could only imagine how embarrassed Jane must have been! That would teach her.

Creeping away into Bonnie's stable, she gave into herself and allowed the laughter to come bursting out. Tears streamed down her face, she laughed so hard. She sank down into a crouched position to avoid being seen. Bonnie turned and put her soft muzzle up to Charlotte's face and began to lick away the tears of joy.

Charlotte stayed in the stable for some time with Bonnie. She noticed how uncomfortable the pony still seemed to be as she edged around her stable. She rubbed her gently and tried to comfort the pony with gentle stroke. Looking at her watch, she decided she had best brave it and head out into the yard if she was going to have her lesson. She poked her head around the corner and saw the yard was clear. Poppy's stable was only metres away, so Charlotte made a quick dash toward it. Looking over the door, she was relieved to see that Poppy had already been tacked up. She wouldn't have to venture any further into the yard and risk bumping into Jane. Quietly, she allowed Poppy to sniff her hand before leading her out into the yard. Poppy walked quietly beside her, so she decided to take the longer way around to the school, hoping that she wouldn't see anyone else.

She did see someone else, Helen. She was hurrying away from the indoor school and towards her. Before Charlotte could begin to wonder why, she called out, "I'll be back in five minutes. I just need to sort something out. Are you OK waiting?" "Yeah I guess so."

Charlotte replied. She wondered what the problem was and hoped it wasn't anything to do with Bonnie. She'd seemed OK when she'd left her only moments ago. Coaxing the little pony on, she made her way into the school. Poppy seemed quiet enough, although Charlotte hoped she wouldn't get impatient about standing around and waiting.

A thought hit her then. She'd pulled off one part of her plan. Now she could pull off the other part: impressing Helen. Carefully, she led the little bay pony over to the mounting block. She was fractionally smaller than Bonnie, probably only about 13hh, although her slight frame made her seem smaller. Taking a deep breath, Charlotte swung herself into the saddle. This was only her fourth time on a pony at Rockingwood, she hoped she wasn't making a mistake. For a second,

Charlotte considered dismounting. She instantly dismissed the thought. Helen wouldn't let her ride a pony that wasn't safe. In fact, she'd be so impressed when she saw that Charlotte had been able to mount by herself.

Poppy stood quietly as Charlotte gathered up the reins, easily remembering how to hold them correctly. Although, she was relieved that the stirrups seemed to be the right length for her, she wasn't sure what she would have done if they hadn't been. Charlotte had been thinking about sitting and waiting for Helen, but she felt so at ease on Poppy, without thinking she nudged her forward into a walk. Poppy automatically went forward and followed the track around the outside edge of the school.

As they reached the far end, Charlotte decided to turn across the diagonal and change the rein. She pulled gently on her inside rein to turn the pony. Poppy didn't respond. Instead, she carried on walking, completely ignoring her rider. Charlotte remembered that Helen had told her before that her reins were always too long. Once she'd shortened them, Poppy responded by turning and walking across the diagonal. Charlotte was really getting the hang of riding by herself now. A grin spread across her face. She thought about urging the pony on into a trot. As she reached the mounting block, she caught sight of Helen coming back toward the school. No, she wouldn't risk being caught trotting now. Instead, she pulled Poppy to a halt by the mounting block. Helen would see her there. Charlotte had no doubt about how impressed she would be!

"Charlotte!" Helen exclaimed as she let herself

through the gate. "What do you think you're doing?"

"I thought I'd be ready for you." Charlotte told her,

beaming.

"You could have been hurt! You don't even know

Poppy!" Helen snapped.

Charlotte didn't know what to say. The last thing she

expected was to make Helen angry. Perhaps she was

better off being honest, "I just wanted to impress you."

"Well maybe think of a safer way next time." Helen

chastised her as she started to examine the pony's tack.

"It's a good job you've only being stood still, the girth is

so loose you could have had a serious accident!"

Charlotte gulped, she'd never even thought to examine

the girth. Never considered the possible consequences.

How could she have

been so stupid? There was no way now that she could tell Helen how she had walked and turned Poppy all by herself. She was already so cross at her.

Even though Helen had been pleasant enough after Charlotte had apologised, Charlotte was sure there was a tension in the air after that incident. The lunge lesson had gone well enough. Better than expected really. Helen had praised her at how much steadier Charlotte had become in the trot already, despite the fact that Poppy had a much choppier trot than Bonnie. In fact, she had been so pleased, that she had allowed Charlotte to have her very first canter on the lunge, holding onto the pommel of the saddle with both hands. Charlotte had felt thrilled as Poppy has surged forward, picking up speed. She'd loved the feeling of the pony's canter.

The thrill was short lived though. It didn't seem right to be too enthusiastic after her earlier stupidity. She was making a real mountain for herself. Not only did she have to avoid Jane and impress Helen, now she had to find a way of proving to Helen that she wasn't totally irresponsible either, if she was to be allowed back to Rockingwood.

Chapter Eleven

Regrets

After Poppy was safely back in her stable, Charlotte had decided to amble over to the outdoor arena. Most of the others had taken a break anyway and headed down to the local shop. Jake was there practising for his upcoming gymkhana competition. He was alone in the school and that suited Charlotte. She leaned against the fence and sighed. Even though she felt down, she couldn't help but marvel at how wonderful it must be for Jake, being allowed to ride by himself in the arena.

With the competition fast approaching, he must be so excited. She thought that he would never do anything stupid or impulsive, like her. Helen probably was thrilled to have him at Rockingwood. Even Jane treated him like an adult and not just some stupid kid. If only she could be a bit more like him.

Jake was once again riding Rosie. The pair charged toward the far end of the arena and Jake took aim to push his flag pole into the top of a cone. He pulled Rosie to a halt and repeated the exercise. He went through the same sequence a number of times, each time becoming better with his aim, before he noticed Charlotte leaning against the gate. He grinned, slipping Rosie a long rein and walking across to where she stood. The pony's dun sides were heaving from the practise.

"Are you hiding there to keep a low profile?" he asked curiously.

Charlotte frowned, was it that obvious? "Umm... How come you're riding Rosie?" she asked, trying to change the subject.

"She's smaller and faster around the tight turns than Penny. I know what you did to Jane. That was some stunt!" She squirmed a little under his stern gaze. How could he possibly know what she had done? No one had seen

her, had they? He looked angry for a while, but

then his face broke into a grin and she breathed a sigh of relief.

"You should have seen her covered in poo!" Charlotte laughed, suddenly sounding delighted. "I'm kind of trying not to bump into her though."

"That won't be too hard." Jake told her. She looked at him quizzically, waiting for him to go on. "She went home. It was quite a nasty knock she had when she fell. Helen was in a right flap that the trailer wasn't safe and with

having to try to get everything organised by herself."

"What?" Charlotte gulped. She couldn't believe what she was hearing. "I only meant to embarrass her. I never even thought she might be injured!" She blurted out.

"Well that's the thing with childish pranks," Jake went on, sounding seriously annoyed, "You just never know if they're going to be funny or have dangerous consequences."

"Does Helen know it was me?" Charlotte suddenly asked.

"No I don't think so." Jake glared.

"Are you going to tell her? Please don't! She'll never allow me back to Rockingwood if she finds out! I'm already in bother!" Charlotte begged, shifting uncomfortably under his glare.

"You're secret's safe with me." Jake assured her, suddenly sounding calmer. "On just one condition." Charlotte raised her eyebrows at this. "You have to apologise to Jane when you see her again." Charlotte gulped. Jake seemed to be enjoying this. He knew she had no choice.

"Yeah alright, I'll do it." She said glumly.

She stayed with Jake for another fifteen minutes, helping him to set up a different combination of gymkhana equipment. It was nearly time for the pony day riders to go home. She knew Jake was right. She had to apologise. But she also knew it would mean she'd never be allowed back to the stables. Jane would simply not allow someone as reckless as her back to the stables. What had she done?

"Once I've un-tacked Rosie, I'm going to turn her out in the paddock. All the mares are out tonight." Jake told her as they left the
 school. "Will you have gone home by then?"
"I was kind of hoping there might be something I could do." Charlotte probed, trying to sound helpful. If she left now, chances were she'd never come back again.
"Well, there's more horses to groom for the evening lessons. How about you make a start on that and when I'm done, I'll follow you around tacking up. We'll need all the hands we can get with Leanne away and Jane having gone home." He told her kindly, he seemed to understand her need to be around the horses.

Charlotte had easily agreed to helping with grooming. Jake had given her a list. She had started with brushing the huge 16.3hh black gelding, Ben. She only hoped she'd managed to remove the dirt from the top of his back – it was just too high for her to see! Ben had turned out to be a gentle giant. After that, she'd brushed Casper, only the little pony had kept nipping at her, annoyed that she was disturbing him whilst he was eating his hay. She'd caught glimpses of Jake dashing back and forth between stables, carrying saddles and bridles.

Finally she had come to groom Sammi. She'd not spent as much time getting to know her best friend's favourite pony as she'd have liked. He was the last on her list to groom, so she supposed she could spend a little more time with him until Jake came around with his tack. Sophie was having her lesson tonight so that she didn't miss out when her family went to the coast for the weekend. If she hung around for a little while longer, she would probably see her. Sophie would be thrilled if Sammi looked extra shiny, so she set about brushing his black coat with the greatest care. Every so often, the beautiful black pony would turn his head toward her and nuzzle her side. His tongue tickled as he licked her hand.

The peacefulness of the moment was disturbed as Carly marched noisily into the little stable block. She must have hung around the stables too.

"Hi." Charlotte greeted her, trying to avoid any more awkwardness.

"Thought you'd have gone home by now." She retorted. She didn't even look at Charlotte, instead she made her way straight to Bonnie's stable, drawing back the bolt and striding inside. Charlotte looked on as she grabbed at Bonnie's head, trying to put her head collar on. The little pony shied away. Carly tried again and this time succeeded. Bonnie was just so honest.

"What are you doing with Bonnie?" Charlotte asked, slightly dismayed at her rough handling.

"Putting her in the field with the other mares." Carly replied moodily.

"Is she allowed? Helen said she's lame."

"I suppose you know everything now you've sucked up to Helen." She sniped. As she saw Charlotte staring at her, she continued, "Look all the mares are going out." With that, she gave Bonnie a sharp tug on the lead rope and dragged the pony out of her stable. Charlotte could only watch in horror as Bonnie limped painfully away.

Chapter Twelve

Help!

Within seconds, Charlotte's mind was spinning. What should she do? Surely dragging Bonnie out to the field when she was clearly in so much pain wasn't right. Then again, this was only the third time in her life that she had been to Rockingwood. Maybe this was how things worked. Maybe Carly had been asked to turn Bonnie out. It just didn't seem right to her. Helen had seemed so concerned earlier. Surely she would want her in the stable so she could keep an eye on her over night. She didn't know what to do, but she had her mind made up. Dashing out of the stables, she was momentarily blinded by the sunlight.

Squinting, she looked around. There was no-one else in sight. She could just see Bonnie's tail disappearing around the corner of the stable yard. At the top of her voice she called out for Jake, but there was no response. She would just have to stop Carly herself.

Sprinting down the yard, she dashed after the pony. As the little roan came into sight, Charlotte drew to a walk so as not to spook her. It was clear now that Bonnie was even lamer than she had first appeared, as she hobbled along the stony path. Charlotte winced. The pony was moving slowly, placing her feet tentatively on the ground. Despite the fact that Carly was pulling on the head collar, Bonnie seemed to be pulling backwards with every stride.

It was then that it hit her. Charlotte stopped in her tracks. Sore feet. The look of rocking backward. Bonnie had laminitis! Charlotte was sure of it. Of course, she had never seen a lame pony before. However, she had read so many pony books, she felt sure that this is what it must be. Her heart felt like it stopped in her chest. If Carly put her out in the field, eating the lush summer grass would make her worse. It could kill her. Charlotte felt tears welling in her eyes. She was more determined than ever now to stop her. It wouldn't be hard to catch them, Bonnie was moving so slowly.

"Carly!" She cried out. "Carly, wait!" A look of annoyance spread over Carly's face as she turned and saw it was Charlotte. Charlotte saw her face and knew she wasn't going to listen. Just like Jane, she thought Charlotte wasn't up to being around horses.

"What now?" Carly grumbled.

"You can't put Bonnie out. Can't you see? She's got laminitis!" Charlotte cried angrily.

"Ha. Like you'd know anything about that. Look Charlotte, you've been around horses for 2 minutes. Just because Helen gave you a lesson it doesn't mean you know everything. Why don't you stop embarrassing yourself! If I were you, I'd spend the summer practising netball. You're going to need the practise if you don't want to look like a fool in September!" Carly smirked and with that she once again tugged on Bonnie's head collar and began to drag her toward the field.

Charlotte stared after them. Fury burnt inside her. How could anyone be so selfish that they'd want to show someone up, with no thought to the pony's welfare. There was only one thing for it; she'd have to

 interrupt the lessons. She didn't care if she embarrassed

herself , she was sure Helen would want to know.

Forcing herself to look away from Bonnie, she

turned and sprinted toward the

 indoor school. Helen should be there by now. She'd

followed Carly the long way around the stable block and

by the time she neared the school, she was breathing

heavily. She could just make out the shape of what

looked like Sammi in the dimness of the indoor school.

Jake must have taken a short cut with him through the

barn. Charlotte caught sight of Sophie's mum by the

viewing gallery. Mrs Scott looked like she was about to

speak to her, but Charlotte just offered her a weak smile

and dashed through the open gateway.

"Charlotte! What on earth are you doing tearing around like this?" Helen chastised her.

 Her voice sounded a little dangerous, but Charlotte wasn't going to let that stop her.

"You've got to come. Quickly!" She gasped, ignoring Helen's question.

"Charlotte?" Helen questioned, raising her eyebrows. "What's going off?"

Charlotte didn't pause as both Helen and Sophie gave her a puzzled look. "It's Bonnie. There's no time to explain. You've got to come." The urgency in Charlotte's voice must have cut through. Before Charlotte knew it, she was leading Helen out of the school. They picked up the pace and began to jog toward the field.

"Why are we going to the paddocks? I thought something was wrong with Bonnie?" Helen asked her between breaths. Before Charlotte could explain, they caught sight of Bonnie. Carly was trying to pull her close enough to open the gate but Bonnie had clearly had enough and didn't look like she wanted to go any further.

Before anyone could say anything, Helen snapped, "What on earth is going on here girls? Charlotte, you knew Bonnie was lame!" Shrinking under Helen's stare, Charlotte suddenly realised that perhaps Helen thought it was her idea to bring Bonnie to the field. Before Carly could twist the truth, she blurted out, "I did. That's why I came. I saw Bonnie had laminitis and Carly was going to put her in the field anyway." She hated accusing people, but it was true. All she could do was hope Helen believed her.

"Don't be so stupid Charlotte. You're just trying to suck up. Of course Bonnie hasn't got laminitis. What would you know!" Carly spat.

"Girls!" Helen cried. Carly looked at the floor, but Charlotte couldn't take her eyes off Bonnie.

Moving forward, Helen gently patted Bonnie on the neck and cooed softly to her. She ran her hand down her front leg and Charlotte noticed that Bonnie was trembling slightly, probably from the effort of walking so far. Her breath seemed heavy too and her sides heaved slightly. Helen had felt her feet and was now pressing her fingers against the inside of her lower leg. She explained that she was feeling for a pulse, as if she could feel one in her leg, it could be a sign of laminitis.

Charlotte held her breath, waiting for the verdict. Jake and Sophie were heading up the field path toward them. Concern was spread across their faces. They didn't speak as they approached, although Charlotte saw the looked of horror spread over Sophie's face as she noticed Carly standing there. Sophie's mouth gaped open and the colour drained from her cheeks. Charlotte could only imagine what she must be feeling, seeing this girl who had made her life a misery for the last year turn up at her stables, but right now they all had to concentrate on Bonnie. After what seemed like an age of silence, Helen stood up.

"I think you're right Charlotte. Bonnie does look like she's got laminitis. We need to get her back to her stable straight away." Helen explained. At hearing this, Carly sighed loudly and began to pull on Bonnie's lead rope, trying to turn her.

"Jake, take Bonnie. Carly I think you've done quite enough damage. I don't know why you thought you knew best when Bonnie is clearly in agony. Wait for me in the tack room while we get this mess sorted out." Helen snapped.

Carly's jaw seemed to drop. "I never even wanted to look after such slow ponies anyway!" She spat, obviously annoyed that Helen was angry with her.

"Slow ponies? What's going off?" Sophie stammered, suddenly finding her voice.

"Carly..." Charlotte was about to explain before being viciously interrupted.

"Me? Ha, it's not me that's such a know it all. All you've done is try to show off all day Charlotte." Carly snapped nastily, "and look at you in those ridiculous jodhpurs, you'll never live this down at school."

Everyone stared, mouths open. Charlotte was for once lost for words. Carly was attacking her and for what? Doing the right thing? Before she could think of anything to say, Sophie unexpectedly stepped in. "It sounds like Charlotte has saved Bonnie's life. I don't know what you're doing here Carly, but you should be grateful to Charlotte." Charlotte didn't know what had gotten into Sophie. She had never seen her stand up to someone before and she was proud of the way she had stepped in to deal with Carly.

Carly didn't look in the slightest bit put off by Sophie's remarks. "Grateful? I don't know who is lamer, the horse or you two!" She bit furiously before turning dramatically on her heel and marching away. Charlotte suspected that would be the last that they would see of her, at Rockingwood at least.

Charlotte turned back to Bonnie and pressed her face into her neck. She was well aware that Sophie was waiting for an explanation as to why Carly was there, but she was trying hard not to cry and didn't want anyone to see that she was upset. Would her beloved pony ever be ok again? A hand

brushed against her back. It was Sophie.

"Don't worry Charlotte, Helen will make sure she's OK. You're a hero. If you hadn't noticed, anything could have happened to her!" Sophie said, smiling kindly at her.

Helen had been on the phone for most of the time that the girls had been talking, but now she turned and asked if the girls had time to wait with Jake and

Bonnie whilst she went to fetch the small horse box. It was a long way to walk back to the stables for a lame pony and she didn't want to take any chances. They both agreed, although Sophie was clearly worrying as her mum would be waiting for her to have her lesson. Still this was more important. Especially as Charlotte had fallen in love with Bonnie, just as she had with Sammi.

Just a few minutes later, Helen was reversing the small horse box up the field path toward them. Sophie offered to hold onto Bonnie's lead rope whilst Jake went to help lower the ramp. Before they started to move Bonnie, Helen offered the pony an apple and explained she had put some pain killer in the middle of it. It wouldn't work for a while, but the sooner she ate it the better. It was a slow and painful job coaxing Bonnie forward and up the low ramp. Each step she took seemed to be more painful than the last.

Sophie and Charlotte took up position on either side of

her, reassuring her and steadying her when necessary.

As soon as she was on board, Helen hopped back in the

cab to drive her back to her stable.

"Can I help you unload her?" Charlotte asked Jake.

"We'll need all the help we can get I think." Jake told

her, sounding glum.

"I'll come too, I'll just nip back to my mum first." Sophie

reassured them as she dashed off toward the school.

For a moment, Charlotte watched her friend disappear.

She couldn't believe how the day had turned out. Sophie

had been kind in calling her a hero. It wasn't true. If it

had been, she would have stopped Carly in the first

place. With a heavy heart, she fell into step beside Jake

and headed back to the stables.

Chapter Thirteen

Ponies at Last!

When Sophie had returned to her mum, she had discovered the other 2 riders in her lesson had decided to postpone until Helen had more time. The riding school was rushed off its feet with Jane being off and Helen needed to make Bonnie a priority. Sophie's mum had suggested she put her lesson on hold too. Of course she understood, but she still felt a little disappointed not to be riding. Her mum had kindly offered to wait so as Sophie could go back and help Charlotte with Bonnie, before giving both girls a lift home.

Sophie found Charlotte by the little stable block, she had a fresh bale of shavings balanced on a wheel barrow. The ramp was already down on the horse box and Helen and Jake were gently encouraging the pony down the ramp. Charlotte gestured for her to follow so she quietly slipped past the lorry and followed Charlotte inside.

"Helen wants us to put a thick shavings bed down for Bonnie. It'll be soft on her feet and she won't be able to eat it." Charlotte explained.

"Ok, if we're quick, we can do it before she's inside." Sophie offered. She was desperate to ask Charlotte about Carly. She couldn't believe that the girl who had made her life so miserable had turned up at the stables. But she bit her lip, now just wasn't the time.

The girls worked just quick enough to have cleared the tools to one side before Bonnie shuffled inside. Helen was right.

Bonnie instantly looked more comfortable once she was stood on the deep, soft shavings. Sophie was sure she saw the pony breathe a sigh of relief. Charlotte didn't look relieved though. She looked as worried as ever.

"What are we going to do?" Charlotte blurted out. Helen glanced toward her and offered a slight smile, "*We* aren't going to do anything. There's nothing more to be done until the vet arrives. I think you've done quite enough for one day Charlotte, don't you?"

If Charlotte didn't look like she might cry before, she did now, "Am I in trouble?" she gulped. At this, Helen let out a slight chuckle that drew a stare from everyone.

"No Charlotte, you're not in trouble!" Helen beamed. "You've worked so hard all day, I don't know what we'd have done without you. And what you've just done for

Bonnie, I can't thank you enough for. If you hadn't noticed or acted so quickly, I dread to think what could have happened." Charlotte's glum face broke into a shy smile at this praise, but before she

could say anything, Helen went on, "It could be hours before the vet arrives, he's already at an emergency on the other side of town. You should go home and get some rest."

"But what about Bonnie?"

"She's already much happier thanks to the cosy bed you girls have made for her. I'll keep an eye on her until the vet arrives. We've caught the laminitis early so hopefully she'll improve quickly." Helen explained.

"How will I know though?" Charlotte asked, a look of sadness creeping onto her face.

Helen looked puzzled, "Know? What do you mean?"

"Know whether Bonnie is OK, I'll never see her again!" Charlotte blurted out, tears clearly welling in her eyes.

"Why ever not?" Helen asked kindly.

"I can't afford to come anymore, my mum saved up so I could come for my birthday."

"Oh." Helen exclaimed and paused, seeming to slip deep into thought. "It doesn't have to cost you that much."

"Even if I didn't come to a pony day and just had a lesson, it'd be too expensive for my mum." Charlotte explained glumly," I'd like to know what happens to Bonnie though."

"I didn't mean you should come for lessons. It'd be a shame not to though, you're a natural rider. Have you ever thought of coming and helping out? We could really do with an extra pair of hands around the place and I'm sure we could stretch to a few free lessons." Helen explained, beaming. Charlotte didn't know what to say. For a moment she was struck speechless, which was rare for Charlotte. Of course she wanted to. YES! YES! She wanted to scream. Only she couldn't. Suddenly, she remembered Jane and what she'd done. Jane would never agree to it,

 especially once she found out that Charlotte was to blame for her accident. "I can't, Jane wouldn't want me here." She explained.

"Now what are you talking about? I know Jane can take a bit of getting used to, but she'd love having someone around here who is really willing to learn. Too many girls just want to ride and not look after the ponies."

Charlotte caught sight of Sophie staring at her.

That was another consideration. Her best friend had

dreamed for so long of helping

 out at the stables, Charlotte wasn't sure she could put

herself before her friend, even though it would be so

painful to miss out on such a fabulous opportunity with

the ponies. This had to be an opportunity for them both.

"What about Sophie, can she help too?" Charlotte asked.

She noticed the look of shock and embarrassment on her

best friend's face, but before she could protest, Helen

had agreed. All they had to do was ask their mum's to

give the final OK to Helen.

        Charlotte couldn't believe it. Her dreams were

coming true. Excitement bubbled through her at the

thought of spending day

after day with the horses. Sophie was grinning

madly too. Charlotte felt a slight twinge of guilt, feeling excited when Bonnie was so ill. At least now, she would be able to spend her time getting her well again.

Carefully, she drew back the bolt and slid into Bonnie's stable. She slipped her arms around the pony's neck and hugged her gently, burying her head in to her pinkish-brown mane.

Chapter Fourteen

All is Well.

It was just 2 days later when Sophie and Charlotte turned up for their first day helping out at Rockingwood. Charlotte's mum had agreed instantly. Sophie's mum had been a little more reluctant, but had agreed knowing that there wasn't anything that would keep her daughter away from the stables now. A good word from Helen over the telephone had helped her to make up her mind. Sophie was worried that something might happen to

change her mother's mind, but she was determined to make sure everything worked out for the best.

Both girls had been relieved when Helen had also let them know that Bonnie had been made more comfortable. The vet had been out and taken x-rays of her feet and given her a supply of pain relief. The farrier was set to come out today and make her a set of special shoes to help her get better. They were both hoping to see the farrier at work, it would be a new experience for them both. The most important thing was that due to Charlotte's quick thinking, Bonnie was going to make a full recovery. It would take a little time, but Helen had assured them that she would be back to her old self soon.

Helen had also told them what had happened with Carly, as no one had seen her since she'd stormed off down the field path. Apparently she had waited in the tack room for Helen, but when Helen had tried to explain to her that she should have asked someone with more experience about what to do with Bonnie, Carly had been furious. She had spitefully told Helen in a rage that she was more experienced than any of the *dumb* helpers at the stables, after all she had been used to riding *proper* ponies, not slow riding school ponies. Helen had remained calm and offered Carly a place on a pony care course about lameness so she could learn more before getting her own pony. This had really tipped Carly over the edge, as she had gone on to inform Helen that her parents would be getting her a much better horse anyway and she didn't need to come to Rockingwood any more, especially when they couldn't see how well she could ride. Somehow Helen had managed to not get angry. She had told her that was fine, before seeing her off of the yard. Charlotte didn't know how anyone could be so rude to an adult. Helen had said that Carly had been spoiled by her parents. Charlotte could see that now. She felt foolish for being taken in by her to start with and thinking she really was experienced with horses. Neither she nor Sophie were looking forward to going back to school and seeing her again. Still that seemed like an age away. They had the whole summer ahead of them at the stables.

As they rounded the corner of the yard, Jake greeted them cheerfully. "Morning, we've been waiting for the hero to return!" He called good-naturedly. Charlotte blushed, she knew he was only joking, but she was no hero. She'd just done the right thing. "Everyone has been talking about you," he carried on, more seriously this time.

"All good I hope!" Charlotte said, laughing nervously. "What do you want us to get started on first?" She asked, trying to change the subject.

"Of course it's all good. Even Jane is thrilled that you did what you did. We're just about to meet in the tack room to share out the jobs for the day." Jake explained, leading the way toward the tack room.

Charlotte gulped and paused in her tracks. Of course she'd known that she'd be seeing a lot of Jane if she was going to help out at Rockingwood. She'd just not planned on doing it so soon. In fact, she'd kind of been hoping to just slip right in, un-noticed. Sophie paused ahead of her, giving her friend a curious look. With all the excitement of the last few days, she'd only briefly mentioned the drama to Sophie. She certainly hadn't mentioned the exact role she had played and how worried she was about getting into trouble. If she had, this would have only caused Sophie to worry even more than she already did.

"Come on Charlotte, what are you waiting for?" Sophie said.

"Um, well..."

Luckily, Jake stepped to the rescue, "Don't worry, I think you've done enough to prove yourself. There's no need now to mention what you did. Turns out Jane caught a bug off Leanne and that's why she went home, it was nothing to do with you."

Charlotte could feel Sophie gawping at her and knew she had some explaining to do later on. Right now, she was just staring at Jake. After a

pause she stammered, "So you aren't going to mention what I did?"

"Are you going to do anything like that again?" He questioned.

"No...no of course I'm not." Charlotte blurted out.

"Then I think that's and end to it, don't you?" He told her good naturedly.

Charlotte could only nod. Relief once again flowed through her. In hindsight, she knew her bid to take revenge on Jane had been childish. She could kind of understand

why they wouldn't want a load of children around the horses if they didn't know what

they were doing. Especially now she'd seen how selfish some of the other girls could be. Just thinking of Carly made her shudder.

She hurried to catch up with the others. Jake offered her a smile as they piled into the tack room. Jane was sat in there on top of a wooden tack box. Leanne was perching on the edge beside her. Charlotte gulped. She knew that at the very least she should clear the air. Suddenly, she didn't feel her usual confident self. Shrinking back slightly into the corner, she tried to make herself feel less exposed.

"Um...hi," she started off rather pathetically, "Look Jane, umm I know you think I'm only

interested in riding, but I really want to learn about looking after the ponies." She babbled, trying to get it off of her chest before she lost her nerve.

A heavy silence hung in the air. Sophie and the others looked awkwardly at the floor, wondering what Jane might say. An uncomfortable moment passed before she finally spoke. "Horse can be dangerous you know. There are enough kids around here who don't respect them enough." She said sternly.

Charlotte turned as white as a sheet, "I know that now, I..." but Jane didn't give her the chance to speak.

"Having said that, you proved you know how to put the horses first. I imagine it was pretty hard for you to stand up to someone like Carly like that." Jane explained, a slight smile appearing on her face.

"I just want to make sure Bonnie is OK." Charlotte offered weakly.

"Well there's a lot more to be done around the Rockingwood than just playing with Bonnie you know. Why don't you start by mucking her stable out? Sophie you could sort Sammi out." Jane instructed.

"Does that mean you're happy for us to stay?" Charlotte asked, looking more hopeful than she had a moment ago.

"Welcome to the team." Jane offered, smiling once again.

Charlotte couldn't believe it. They had been accepted here at Rockingwood, even by Jane. One of the team she had said! "We won't let you down!" She called over her shoulder as she linked arms with Sophie and the two girls dashed off toward the stables.

Charlotte with Bonnie, the magical strawberry roan and Sophie with her beloved

Sammi, this was just the start of their adventure. It had seemed impossible only weeks ago, but now they were going to live their dream with their ponies at last.

Quiz Time

1. How did Sophie win a second place rosette?

2. What was the name and breed of Charlotte's mum's horse?

3. How big is Rosie?

4. What breed is Penny?

5. What was Sammi's favourite place to scratch?

6. How big is Sammi?

7. What did Sammi do when he should have been waiting for Eddie to canter?

8. What did Sophie get Charlotte for her birthday?

9. How did Charlotte's mum surprise her on her birthday?

10. What job did the girls have to do on the pony day that they hadn't planned for?

11. Why could Sophie not ride Sammi on the hack out?

12. Who did Sophie and Charlotte make friends with at the stables?

13. Who turned up unexpectedly at the stables?

14. How did Charlotte first notice Bonnie had laminitis?

15. How did Helen check Bonnie for signs of laminitis?

1. In a quiz in her pony magazine

2. A welsh cob called Ted

3. 14.2 hands high

4. A thoroughbred

5. His withers

6. 13 hands high

7. He galloped off around the school

8. A riding lesson

9. She booked her two full pony days at the stables

10. Mucking out

11. He was naughty because he liked to buck and gallop off

12. Jake and Leanne

13. Carly Johnson

14. Her feet appeared to be sore and she looked like she

was rocking backward

15. She felt the bottom of Bonnie's leg to see if there

was a pulse.

Bay: A horse with a brown body and black mane, tail and points (the lower legs). There can be bright bays, with golden brown coats, or dark bays, with dark brown coats.

Black: A horse who is genuinely black, only has black hairs. A horse with some dark brown hairs should be classed as dark bay.

Chestnut: A horse with a ginger-red coat. A bright chestnut has a bright coat, whilst a liver chestnut is much darker in colour.

Coloured: Coloured horses can be piebald or skewbald. Piebald means that the horse is black and white, whilst skewbald means that the horse is brown and white.

Dun: A horse with a sandy coloured coat and dark brown or black mane, tail and points. Dun horses normally have a black dorsal stripe running down the centre of their back.

Strawberry Roan: Also known as red roan. An unusual colour, where the coat is a mixture of chestnut and white hairs. The mane, tail and points can be a solid colour.

19954672R00129

Printed in Great Britain
by Amazon